# What Every Good Lawyer Wants You To Know

An Insider's Guide on How to Reduce Stress,
Reduce Costs and Get the Most From Your Lawyer

**FRANCINE R. TONE, Esq.**

Published by Torii Publishing

P.O. Box 34045 | Truckee, California 96160
Phone: (530) 582-9877
Email: info@ToriiPublishing.com
www.ToriiPublishing.com

Copyright © 2016 Francine R. Tone. All rights reserved.

All rights reserved. No part of this book may be used or reproduced by any means, graphic, electronic, or mechanical, including photocopying, recording, taping or by any information storage retrieval system without the express permission of the publisher except in the case of brief quotations embodied in critical articles and reviews.

Because of the dynamic nature of the internet, any links or web addresses contained in this book may have changed since publication and may no longer be valid.

The views expressed in this book are solely those of the author and do not necessarily reflect the views of the publisher and the publisher hereby disclaims any responsibility for them.

Without limiting the rights under the copyright law reserved above, no part of this publication may be reproduced or transmitted in any form or by any means whatsoever without the written permission of the publisher.

This publication is intended to provide accurate and authoritative information in regard to the subject matter covered based on the experiences and perception of the author. However, none of the information contained in this publication is intended, implied and represented to be legal advice in any manner whatsoever. Anything suggested by an attorney or legal representative to a client should reign superior to any statements or presentations made in this book.

There may be mistakes, typographical and in content. Neither author nor publisher shall have liability or responsibility to any person or entity with respect to any loss or damage caused, or allegedly to have been caused, directly or indirectly, by the information contained in this book.

First Edition 2016
E-Kindle ISBN: 978-0-9980687-0-1
Paperback ISBN: 978-0-9980687-1-8
Printed in the United States of America

# To Jeffry

My life and law partner—thank you for your unconditional support.

# Table of Contents

Forward ............................................................................................... 9
Acknowledgments .......................................................................... 11
I. Introduction ................................................................................. 13
II. How to Use This Book ............................................................... 23
III. Your Good Lawyer .................................................................... 25
    Do You Need a Lawyer? ............................................................ 26
        Preventive Law ...................................................................... 26
        Legal Advice or Legal Information ................................... 27
    Finding a Lawyer ...................................................................... 29
        Referrals First ........................................................................ 30
        All Other Methods ............................................................... 31
        Credentials ............................................................................. 32
    Traits of a Good Lawyer ........................................................... 32
        Experience ............................................................................. 33
        Presence ................................................................................. 34
        Communication .................................................................... 34
        Empathy ................................................................................. 34
        Boundaries ............................................................................. 35
        Time ........................................................................................ 35

    Instinct .................................................................................................. 35
    Red Flags ............................................................................................. 36
    Questions & Conversations ............................................................... 36
  Fee Agreements ........................................................................................ 38
    Types of Fee Agreements ................................................................... 40
    Costs ..................................................................................................... 41
    Trust Accounts .................................................................................... 42

## IV. Things to Know about the Legal System ............................................ 45
  Why Do Lawsuits Take So Long? ........................................................... 46
    Court System ....................................................................................... 46
    Court Calendars .................................................................................. 48
    Multiple Calendars ............................................................................. 48
    Time ..................................................................................................... 49
    Technology .......................................................................................... 50
  Show Me | Show Me | Show Me ............................................................. 50
    Show Me the Money ........................................................................... 51
    Show Me the Facts ............................................................................. 53
    Show Me the Evidence ...................................................................... 55
  Professionalism ........................................................................................ 56
    Lawyer's Reputation in Court ........................................................... 56
    Lawyer's Reputation in the Community ......................................... 58
  Case Resolution ........................................................................................ 59
    Settlement ............................................................................................ 60
    Early Settlement and ADR ................................................................ 62
    Our Case is a Slam Dunk! ................................................................. 63
  How Much Do We Get or Have to Pay? ............................................... 64
    Punitive Damages ............................................................................... 64
    Contract Damages .............................................................................. 66
    Other Damages ................................................................................... 67

| | |
|---|---|
| Other Things to Consider | 68 |
|     Leave Drama for TV & Movies | 68 |
|     The Law is Wrong! | 69 |
|     Fault v. Injury | 70 |
| **V. Things You Can Do** | **73** |
|     Re-Read Chapter IV | 74 |
|     Think Settlement: REALLY! | 74 |
|     Discuss Objectives and Motivation | 75 |
|     Set Communication Ground Rules | 76 |
|     Seriously Assume Your Role as Client | 77 |
|         Decision-Making | 77 |
|         Prepare Your Facts | 77 |
|         Organize Your Documents | 79 |
|         Stay Organized | 81 |
|         Just Answer the Question PLEASE! | 81 |
|         Be Courteous | 83 |
|         Opposition | 84 |
|     Beware The Over-Traps | 85 |
|         Over-Researching | 86 |
|         Over-Thinking | 87 |
|         Over-Discussing | 88 |
| **VI. Conclusion** | **91** |
| **Appendix** | **93** |
|     Resources | 94 |
|     Lawyer's Code of Ethics | 95 |
| **Glossary** | **97** |
| **About the Author** | **105** |

# Forward

I have been practicing law for over forty-five years, and I like to think of myself as one who is very sensitive to the experience of the legal process from the client's point of view.

I, like most good lawyers, firmly believe in preparing my clients at the beginning of my representation for the difficulties inherent in legal processes. Nonetheless, it so very often happens that something, or several things, occurs during a matter which causes difficulties. Perhaps they arise from the inherent limits of the system itself; perhaps they arise from the methods and strategies I employ in pursuing my client's interests; perhaps they arise from the client's own attitudes toward their own case or the opposing party.

For example, when a client learns that his or her lawyer has granted a second extension of the legal deadline to opposing counsel to produce documentary evidence, if the client is not at least "primed" to know that these things frequently occur, or that there are time, cost and strategic considerations to enforcing strict compliance, the client may immediately feel that his or her lawyer is not diligently pursuing the case or is not "tough enough." If the client is already feeling that way before hearing the lawyer's explanation of the particular situation, such explanations may sound more like "excuses," needlessly undermining the lawyer-client relationship.

We cannot cover every potential aspect of a client's matter at the beginning of the case. This book serves as a primer and should be required reading before a lay person seeks the assistance of an attorney to address legal issues. By being better prepared for the experience of going through the legal process, you, the client will be in a position to better "hear" what your lawyer explains to you along the way; you will be in a position to stress less over the inevitable frustrations; and, you will be in a position to assist your lawyer more in pursuing and protecting your cause, and thus save costs.

Francine Tone is an experienced California attorney with many years of experience in the trial courts and at the appellate court level. I consider myself a contributor to Ms. Tone's work over the years on these client issues, as I am one of the many lawyers who often pick up the phone and call Tone & Tone when wrestling with a decision as to the direction in which to take a case. Her experience in guiding other lawyers in the very issues covered in this book makes her particularly suited to "prime" you for your legal experience. With these qualifications, Francine has described the potential pitfalls and she has addressed the questions that a prospective litigant may encounter in the maze that is our legal system.

This book should be in the library of every good lawyer and should be frequently reviewed by a good lawyer. Even a good lawyer may become insensitive to the concerns of the client. It is important for a good lawyer to recognize that the client is entering unknown territory and the legal concepts and procedures that are second nature to the good lawyer constitute a foreign language to the client. Presenting a prospective client with this book would be an important first step in representing the client. It will go far to establish the trust and confidence that every client should have in his or her lawyer.

Sincerely,

Grace Kubota Ybarra, Esq.
*Attorney at Law*

# Acknowledgments

Writing a book in the midst of managing a law practice turned out to be quite a challenge. I did take the advice of an experienced and sage author and wrote from beginning to end without trying to edit the book while I wrote. That was good advice. Otherwise the book may never have been written. But when editing began, the real work began. I have re-organized the materials numerous times while adding and subtracting so much text. It was hard when my editors suggested cutting out entire sections of what I thought was well-written literature. (I say this with tongue in cheek.) But the hours spent editing has been worthwhile. None of this would have been possible without the help of several people who supported me along the way.

Jeffry, my husband, my law partner, and my life partner, this book would never have been written without your unconditional support and love. Thank you for encouraging me to write it. Thank you for encouraging me to continue when it was tough. Thank you for your collaboration, advice, and thoughtfulness in every aspect of the process, in the writing of the words and in delivering the message. I could not have done this without you.

Grace Kubota Ybarra, Esq., a friend and colleague, who has been the source of tremendous support in life as well as in my practice as a lawyer, thank you for years of wisdom and support.

Christina Nemec and Chase Rogers of Simply Worded (www.simplyworded.com), thank you both for reading through the book in its many forms and providing sound editing advice. Your wisdom and experience were invaluable in delivering the product and message with consistency.

Chase Rogers, thank you for your design direction in fashioning the perfect cover for the book.

Simone Janssen, thank you for your encouragement to leave comfort behind and take on an adventure that often left me standing at the precipice.

Jason Jordan, thank you for your guidance. Thank you for asking the right questions to make sure my message was being delivered.

# I. Introduction

*"All truths are easy to understand once they are discovered; The point is to discover them."*

GALILEO GALILEI

A number of years ago, my husband and I were sued. It was a lawsuit by our former partners over the break-up of our law practice. Upset, worried, and angry, I knew we had to find a good lawyer. To my surprise, I discovered that we had become deeply emotionally invested in the case. But we were lucky; we had access to many lawyers and knew the ropes. Or, so I thought.

Of course, we wanted someone we could work with and be able to trust completely. Obviously, we wanted a competent lawyer who was well-versed in the law and who knew the facts. But we also needed someone astute enough to bring us back to reality when we got too caught up in the strife. We needed someone who would tell us not to worry when we were succumbing to anger, frustration, and anxiety. We wanted the freedom to express our ideas and have them considered earnestly. We wanted someone to understand how difficult it was for us to feel out-of-control.

Thankfully, through our built-in referral system based on our experience with many lawyers, we found that lawyer. That lawyer was a former opponent with whom we had battled in several cases. He stayed the course when we were swerving. As unsettling as this role-reversal was, we knew we had to trust our lawyer if we were going to get through this. We also knew we had to be prepared and open-minded to use our lawyer most efficiently. We also knew that to get what we wanted was not going to be cheap. Lawyers are expensive. There is no "standard" fee for what lawyers charge. The cost of legal services is generally high. We don't see that changing much. But, the information in this book will give you more knowledge and power to help control some of that cost.

There were things that our lawyer outlined, combined with our own legal experience, that helped us navigate this challenging, expensive lawsuit. We did everything the lawyer asked us to do. We organized our facts and documents. Even though we understood the process, we listened attentively to what our lawyer was telling us as if hearing it for the first time. We were the client. We had to take certain steps towards a desirable outcome, and only our lawyer could steer us there. Because we heeded our lawyer's advice, we saved money as well as unnecessary grief and stress.

When the lawsuit was done (we settled), I was relieved it was all over. Looking back, I can now appreciate what clients go through as my experience was, from start to finish, disruptive. I could see that doing the things I outline for you in this book reduced my stress and mitigated my costs. I was able to truly value the lawyer I hired. My goal is to help you avoid some of the pitfalls as well as make best use of your legal counsel.

## Becoming a Lawyer

Before I went to law school, I worked as a legal secretary for two exemplary women lawyers. Both had become lawyers as a second career, and both were well past 40 when they graduated from law school. I watched these women run a successful business while fighting hard for the rights of their clients. They took on the police in a civil rights case. They took on the welfare department on behalf of a welfare recipient. They took on banks that were oppressing small businesses. They advocated for women and children in family court. They represented landlords when the tenants did not pay. They counseled both the fortunate and not so fortunate individuals and businesses. The common thread was that they cared about their clients, every single one of them. This impressed me.

Later, I worked as a paralegal for a law office in which a lawyer represented a foreclosure trustee. This trustee was getting sued repeatedly in the early 1980s, the heyday of foreclosures and foreclosure litigation. I observed a lawyer who worked hard every day, all day. He was an expert on foreclosure law, yet he researched the law all the time and poured through files with extreme diligence. He was always in trial. I had the privilege of witnessing our hard work in the office (preparation, preparation, preparation) play out in the courtroom. I was hooked.

By the time I decided to go to law school, I had some idea of what I would do when I graduated. Law school was nothing like what I envisioned.

I quickly learned that anywhere from 20-50% of those who began law school would not finish. *I hoped I would not be in that group.* Then I learned that memorizing information did not benefit me. The law professors used the Socratic methods, and my first answers to questions did not seem to matter to them—even when I knew I was right! This method of teaching was different than most of my prior schooling. It presented a thrilling challenge.

What I learned was that the primary function of law school is to teach students to "think like a lawyer." When a law professor asks a law student a question and the student answers—even correctly, the professor does not accept the answer. Instead, the professor will ask another probing question, and then another, then another. As a result, the student becomes dumbfounded until realizing there are underlying assumptions which must be analyzed and accepted or rejected before knowing the ultimate "right" answer.

Over time, this exercise trains the mind to dig deeper and never accept what appears true to be the final truth. A lawyer is trained not only to turn over every stone, but to check every crevice in the stone and the dirt beneath. This critical approach, which has been painstakingly developed in law school, is at the heart of what a lawyer needs to be successful. And this is what you will look for in a lawyer—as maddening as it can be.

∼

Those who finish law school are equipped with the fundamental ideals exemplified by the profession. The Law was created to defend and uphold ideals that make any society secure. In fact, at every law school graduation, someone will speak to the graduating class and mention the noble art of lawyering.

> *"And make no mistake:*
> *no profession is more honorable than law.*
> *The defenders of the Constitution,*
> *the guardians of our liberty,*
> *the advocates of just causes,*
> *no matter how unpopular,*
> *the protectors of the powerless,*
> *the wise counselors of our society*
> *– that is the role of America's lawyers."*
>
> BOB WRIGHT, UNIVERSITY OF VIRGINIA
> SCHOOL OF LAW GRADUATION 2002

I heard a similar speech at my graduation, and I truly believed it. I still do in spite of some of the malpractice out there. In my profession, I have met a lot of lawyers, *the good, the bad, and the ugly*. I discovered that the good lawyers believe what I believe. They believe that lawyers exist to help people and make sure our system of law continues to work for people. These ideas are promoted through continuing education courses and seminars. Even when day-to-day life drags us through the hills and valleys of disputes and difficulties, we are still members of a noble profession. Sometimes lawyers don't spend enough time thinking about these ideals because we get caught up in the day-to-day. The hope is that you find, or have found, a lawyer whose intentions are noble and ethics are strong. This book will help. Because from what I have seen during the past 40 years, I know that good lawyers truly care about what happens to their clients.

Despite my beliefs, however, once I began practicing law, I learned something else about being a lawyer. Some lawyers can be motivated by money instead by the desire to help clients, and legal combat can override the desire to solve problems. We lawyers do hate to lose. Realities of how some lawyers practice overshadow the noble ideals that good lawyers believe. I have seen some lawyers drive toward making more money and use combat to do so. When I see one of those lawyers taking on a case, I often see their clients mimicking and adopting the same attitudes. The results of these tactics can be devastating to clients, their pocketbooks, and their lives. Those lawyers would not fit the definition of a "good" lawyer as outlined in this book. Those clients are never served as well as they could be. When opposed by one of those lawyers, even a good lawyer will have difficulty keeping your costs and stress down.

But you, as a client, have some control over how your legal matter is handled by hiring a good lawyer and understanding what it means to be "a good" client.

## What Makes "A Good" Client

Our firm handles business and real estate transactions and lawsuits. For over 40 years, we have represented entrepreneurs, real estate brokers and agents, buyers and sellers of real estate, lessors and lessees of commercial property, business and real estate aspects of divorces, probate/estate planning cases, and other specialty areas as well as appeals from these areas. Today, our firm continues to represent business owners and entrepreneurs. I personally handle appellate work. As an appellate lawyer, I see clients after they have gone through an ordeal in the trial court after being represented by other lawyers. Someone has already won or lost, and now the person who lost is challenging the results. Sometimes the challenger comes to me. Sometimes the person defending the result comes to me.

Over the past 40 years, I have had many opportunities to talk to clients we represented along with those represented by other lawyers. This has provided me with some insight into who clients are and what they are going through.

So, I began considering what made a client a "good" client. It was not because he/she brought a good case or paid fees on time. Working with that particular client was simply more comfortable. I considered why, in equally demanding cases with similar results, some clients fared better than others. I considered why some clients seemed to get in the way of their own cases. I began exploring these issues with other lawyers. The genesis of this book arose from our many conversations and observations.

After examining why some clients were more comfortable to work with than others, I came to realize that the client who had it easiest was the one who intuitively understood the information provided in this book and who was open to receive guidance from his/her lawyer. But the clients who were the least satisfied were less informed and less inclined to heed the counsel of their lawyers.

This book is not about "The Top 10 Secrets to Winning a Lawsuit." The plain truth is that in the everyday world of legal cases—whether in a lawsuit, out of court disputes or business dealings requiring lawyers—what dominates the end result is the actual strength of a client's position. A good lawyer will tell you honestly the strength of your position.

The surest way that clients can best weather their experience (and perhaps advance their own cases to get preferable results) stems from their willingness to learn and be proactive. Additionally, this book is about what every good lawyer *wants you to know*, so you can be empowered while minimizing stress and costs. It will assist you in getting the best counsel from your lawyer.

A colleague with whom I have discussed these issues over the years once put it to me very succinctly. He said, "Sometimes, the next worst thing to losing a lawsuit is winning one." I hope here to help you avoid that conundrum.

When I was the client in that lawsuit, I was fortunate because I had found a good lawyer. He also happened to be someone we had *vehemently* opposed on two previous cases. Though we may have disagreed in a lawsuit, I recognized him to be an outstanding lawyer. But my lawyer was also fortunate because, despite my anxiety and my tendency to get pulled off track (as all litigants are inclined to do when it is their personal stake in the game), I was at least *primed* to hear everything he had to say to me along the way. This is what I am now offering to you in this book.

When we were preparing for depositions, he saw my anger flare. He reminded me that the deposition was not the place to argue my case. He encouraged me to "just answer the questions." When we were having discussions about the settlement, I pointed out what I thought was "indisputable" evidence proving the other side wrong. He wisely reminded me that despite what we might prove, we had to do a risk-cost-benefit analysis of prolonging the fight. He held me together.

In the long run, I reduced stress. I reduced costs. My good lawyer guided me to a reasonable resolution I could easily live with.

∼

> *"Trust is the glue of life.*
> *It's the most essential ingredient in*
> *effective communication.*
> *It's the foundational principle*
> *that holds all relationships."*
>
> STEPHEN COVEY

Although you might think that the best time for the lawyer to tell you everything in this book is at the beginning of the representation, it probably isn't. At the beginning of the case, you will be concerned with finding a lawyer and making sure he/she is the right one. You will be concerned about fees and focused on the outcomes. If a lawyer told you everything in this book at that first meeting, you probably would be overwhelmed and remember very little. But a good lawyer will share everything as needed.

This book was written so you would have this information at your fingertips at the beginning. Reading this information, you will be *primed* to *hear* your good lawyer and can repeatedly re-educate yourself.

The information in this book is not exclusive of other things a lawyer might want you to know. But by reading this book, you will be ready to hear whatever else your lawyer might tell you. Your good lawyer may add to the topics in this book because your lawyer will be dealing with the specifics of your case. My suggestion is that you use this book as a place to write down the extra things your lawyer tells you.

Finally, the reality is you *have* to trust your lawyer. You don't have any choice. I cannot suggest that you trust just any person or just any lawyer.

Once you have found a good lawyer you can trust, my wish for you is that you and your lawyer will together work through your problem and that your relationship with your lawyer will be as good at the end of the case as it was at the beginning.

The purpose of this book is to provide you with an understanding of what every good lawyer wants you to know. It is a primer for your mind to be ready to receive information from your lawyer. Now let's get started!

# II. How to Use This Book

*"Begin at the beginning," the King said, very gravely, "and go on till you come to the end; then stop."*

Lewis Carroll, Alice in Wonderland

You will get the greatest benefit by reading this book from beginning to end. As the King suggests don't read it in a rush. Take time to digest the information. Write notes in the margins or in the note section in the back of this book. Make notations in the book about information your lawyer shares with you. By writing in this book, you will likely retain more of the information and be able to put it to better use.

This book is a guide that will hopefully provide you with a better legal experience. This book is not a substitute for getting legal advice. This book contains information that relates to your lawyer-client relationship and what your good lawyer wants you to know. This book does *not* contain legal advice.

When you ask a lawyer a general question, the lawyer's answer almost always is "it depends." This is an honest answer because every legal issue depends on so many factors: the precise facts and the precise law that applies to those facts. It is the lawyer's job to know which facts are critical and which ones are not. Then the lawyer conducts research to find the law that applies to those critical facts. As the lawyer learned through the Socratic methods in law school, he or she looks at every stone and checks "every crevice in the stone and the dirt beneath."

Nor is this book suggesting that a bad case plus a good lawyer equals a win. A bad case is one in which the facts in your case combined with the applicable law do not allow you to have the results you want. Either your position is simply not right, or the law is just against you. No matter how good your lawyer is, he or she will not win a bad case. But, if you have a bad case, your lawyer will do his or her best to reduce your loss. You will still reduce stress, reduce costs, and get the most from your good lawyer.

# III. Your Good Lawyer

> *"At the most pragmatic level, lawyers are society's professional problem solvers".*
>
> Rennard Strickland & Frank T. Read

This book was written under the assumption that you have hired or will hire a good lawyer. A good lawyer is someone who is honest, ethical, professional, and experienced in the area of law pertinent to your case.

This book parallels much the same information a good lawyer should convey.

A good lawyer will tell you directly what you need to hear, not what you want to hear. If you just want someone to tell you what you want to hear, you do not need a good lawyer. Anyone will do.

In looking for a good lawyer, you are looking for someone you can be comfortable with. You will be working with this person for quite some time. You want someone you can trust with your personal information. You want to have the confidence that he/she will be looking out for your best interests at all times during the relationship.

# Do You Need a Lawyer?

## Preventive Law

*"An ounce of prevention is worth a pound of cure."*

Benjamin Franklin

Sometimes the best time to see a lawyer is when nothing bad is happening. Preventive Law can reduce future problems and, in some cases, eliminate them. It is always cheaper for a lawyer to look at your situation in advance and help you take steps to avoid future problems than it is for a lawyer to fix a problem.

Here is an example of someone who waited too long to retain a lawyer. Dave used to purchase small shopping centers that needed renovating for resale. The first time Dave came to our office was because his latest purchase was running into problems, and the seller was not cooperating. We looked over Dave's documents and realized that the seller was not responding because the seller probably thought the problem was all Dave's responsibility. Some of the language in Dave's contract was unclear. One person might read it and say it was all Dave's problem. Another might read it and say it was seller's problem. Because the seller would not communicate, Dave's only recourse was to file a lawsuit. Eventually the case settled. But Dave had to settle for less and spent over $50,000 in attorney's fees.

We told Dave that if he was going to enter into these contracts regularly, he might consider having a lawyer review the contracts before he signed to avoid repeating this scenario. Dave was a sharp dealmaker, but he didn't know how to write legally tight contract provisions. Dave didn't take our advice. About a year later, Dave came to us again with a similar situation and again spent over $50,000 in fees to fix it. Dave stated he didn't want to spend the money up front. We told him any lawyer would charge probably $1,000 to $1,500 to look over a contract, and that seemed less costly than spending $50,000 for even one broken deal. It took Dave nearly five years to learn this lesson. Finally, one day, Dave appeared with an unsigned contact in hand. We reviewed it for $1,000. Dave had no more problems and saved himself a great deal of money.

Whether or not you seek legal advice depends on what is at risk. The more money that is at stake, the more likely some legal advice in advance could save you money down the road.

## Legal Advice or Legal Information

**Legal advice** comes directly from a lawyer. **Legal information** can come from many sources and be found almost anywhere. The key is in knowing the difference. Unfortunately, the line between advice and information is not always clear. I hope to provide you with some insight here that will clarify this.

**Legal advice** comes from a most reliable source—your lawyer. Your lawyer has the education, skills, and experience to analyze your situation and determine what makes your case unique. He/She offers insight that will guide your decisions. How you respond to that advice will have an effect on your rights and obligations. And perhaps most importantly and a significant reason why you go to a lawyer, he/she has undertaken duties to assure that the advice is accurate, reasonable, and consistent with the law as it applies to your situation. *Legal advice is advice on the course of action a person should take to advance or protect his/her best interests.*

Some examples requiring legal advice include:

1. What is your opinion on [fill in the blank]?
2. What do I put on this form?
3. How do I hold title to this real estate?

4. Should I sign this contract?
5. How can I make the co-owner of property sell it?
6. What can I do when someone who owes me money doesn't pay?
7. What can I do when my new car's engine blows up?
8. Can I let my dogs out to attack a trespasser on my land?
9. How do I word the paragraph in the contract to say [fill in the blank]?
10. I think I've been wronged; how can I determine if I'm correct, and what can I do?

And the list goes on.

So when you get "advice" from your family, friends, plumber, real estate agent, escrow officer, banker, doctor, accountant, notary public, etc., that is not legal advice. Even if they say, "the law says …," it is not legal advice. And sometimes what you hear may be correct, but often what you hear is incorrect and will always be incomplete. I strongly recommend you not act on what sounds like legal advice from anyone but a lawyer.

**Legal information**, on the other hand, is readily accessible and general. I have heard and seen writings that try to distinguish legal advice by answering questions that start with "should I" or "whether" while legal information is that which answers "who, what, when, where, and how." I think this is too simplistic and misleading. I purposely included questions above that started with "what" and "how" to illustrate the point. But if you can start your questions with "should I" or "whether," it is a pretty good clue that you are asking for legal advice, not legal information. Some examples of questions calling for legal information include:

1. Where is the correct place to go to file [fill in the blank]?
2. Are these the forms I use to file a lawsuit for [fill in the blank]?

3. What are the steps I need to take to get a lawsuit filed?
4. How much do I have to pay to file the lawsuit?
5. Can I file this claim in small claims court?

Many courts' and bar associations' websites provide large amounts of general information. What you find on those websites is what I would refer to as reliable legal information.

Assuming you have determined your need for legal advice, looking for and reviewing legal information that may be related to your situation can be useful in preparation for meeting your lawyer.

## Finding a Lawyer

Our firm does not aggressively advertise. Our phone number is listed on our website and found in the phone book. The last name starts with "T" so we aren't on the short list of immediate phone calls. Yet, we marvel at the number of cold calls we do get. And when we ask them how they obtained our number, the answer is "the phone book" or "the internet." Our first reaction is to tell the caller, "first piece of free advice: don't pick your lawyer from the phone book or on the internet!" Typically, the calls involve matters that we do not handle, and so we become the first reliable referral for the caller—a good start for this caller.

I personally believe that lawyers should have websites. It offers a resource for clients to find out more about the lawyer and the law firm before hiring the lawyer. But, I do not believe it is the best source for finding the lawyer initially.

So how *do* you find a lawyer? In level of *importance* and *reliability*, here's what you do.

## Referrals First

There are times I needed to find a window washer or a plumber. I do not look at the phone book or internet as my first resource. I call my friends for referrals. I want the name of the person my friends say was fair, honest and reliable. If I'm looking for a doctor, I get a referral from my doctor. I don't search on the internet first. Once I have a name, I may begin researching the person a bit on the internet—just to make sure that person does not have a lot of negative reviews. I'm sure you do likewise. So when looking for a lawyer, certainly do no less.

It is my firm opinion that searching for your lawyer through referrals is the only responsible way to find your good lawyer. It will involve some work on your part, but if you have a situation serious enough to require a lawyer, you need to roll up your sleeves and get cracking.

If you have ever used a good lawyer in the past, regardless of his/her area of law, call that lawyer to get referrals for those who do practice in the area of need. Next contact people you know to be reliable and responsible. You don't even have to know them very well. Ask for the names of lawyers they respect and with whom they have had a satisfactory experience. Even if their lawyer does not practice in the field you need, get the information anyway.

Someone may tell you, "I don't really know any lawyers, but my boss deals with lawyers all the time. You can ask him." Do so. Someone will tell you that their estate planning lawyer was great; call that lawyer because he may know someone who practices in the area you need and can refer you. Whenever you move on to the next contact, drop the name of the person who referred you. Everyone likes referrals, and it's polite to acknowledge the person who referred you. This may sound a bit hit-and-miss, but if you pursue a number of lines of inquiry, you will zero in on good lawyers. How do you know when to stop? You stop when your instincts tell you that you can trust the lawyer sitting across the desk from you, and when you know that person has the traits of a good lawyer.

During your investigation, you will probably hear about some "not-so-good" lawyers. Ask about them, too. You may learn what to avoid.

This is by far the best method by which you can evaluate and choose any lawyer. Use referrals and go with your gut.

## All Other Methods

**Certified Lawyer Referral Services.** Many state and bar associations have referral services with a list of local lawyers. There is usually a screening process so that the lawyers on the panel meet minimum requirements. Most of these referral services have websites now, and you can learn about the program before calling them. By using this method, the first lawyer you see will have at least some experience in the area of law you need. So if you have a real estate problem, you will get the name of a real estate lawyer. If your real estate problem is in a specific subcategory, the referral service will be able to give you the name of a lawyer in that subcategory. For example, if your real estate problem involves getting evicted, the referral service can give you the name of a lawyer who handles landlord/tenant disputes.

Before you meet with your potential lawyer, review the "Interviewing Your Lawyer" section. And if for any reason you feel this is not the right lawyer for you, don't be hesitant to ask him/her for a referral. Or, go back to the referral service. Remember, you must be willing to work to find your lawyer.

**Advertisements.** There are many lawyers who choose to advertise in the Yellow Pages, on billboards, radio, or television. I know you have seen some of these ads. Lawyers are allowed to advertise as long as the advertisements do not contain false or misleading information. Just remember, though, advertisements are a solicitation for business, not a source for reliable information. However, just because a lawyer advertises, it does not mean a lawyer is bad. I know several colleagues who happen to advertise. It's just not the place to start unless you have nowhere else to begin. But if seeing a lawyer who does advertise gives you a starting point (and you never know), that lawyer may end up being *your* good lawyer.

**The Internet.** Technological advancements over the last 25 years leave no question that people often go to the internet first to find anything and everything, including lawyers. Before the internet, the Yellow Pages used to be where some lawyers would "advertise" more information. Websites have replaced the Yellow Pages. A person can write even more now because there is no one-page limitation. In my opinion, websites are multi-paged advertisements.

I don't see anything wrong with lawyers having websites. We have one for our practice. The benefit of a website is, of course, that more information can be offered. My point is that websites contain legal information, not legal advice.

## Credentials

While you are in the process of looking for a lawyer, make sure you are looking in your state or local area. A lawyer has to be licensed in the state to which the advice relates. For example, I am licensed in the State of California to practice law. I can give legal advice for matters in California (including federal courts) but not for any other state. Sometimes people aren't sure which state is involved. For example, you may live in California, and someone else lives in Utah. You have a dispute. Which lawyer do you call? A California lawyer or a Utah lawyer? That depends on the circumstances of the case. You can first call a lawyer in your state.

∼

## Traits of a Good Lawyer

Now that you have a list of some lawyers to call, the next step is to begin interviews. Your first appointment is just like a job interview. You are determining if this lawyer can handle your case and if this is the right fit for your situation and personality. Is this person trustworthy? Understand that the lawyer is also interviewing you to determine if he/she wants you for a client. The lawyer is also deciding if your case is worth handling. You both want to make sure that this is the right fit.

Have an honest discussion and express all of your concerns upfront. Lawyers understand that hiring a lawyer is a major commitment by a client. We know you are looking for someone who will take care of your situation, answer your questions, and give you some sense of comfort that someone highly qualified is working for you. We know that some clients need a little more hand holding than others. We know that you need to know that the lawyer is on your side. The only way for you to be assured that you have found the right person is to have an open and honest discussion with your lawyer. Do not be afraid to say what is on your mind. We'd rather hear about what concerns you have as soon as possible. If your concerns cannot be addressed, the lawyer will say so and give you a referral. Below, I have included some basic areas that you should discuss and assess, so you can spot a good lawyer.

## Experience

Does the lawyer have experience in the relevant field? If you have a real estate problem, you want a real estate lawyer. But even that category may be too broad. For example, if you have a landlord-tenant issue, you want a real estate lawyer that handles landlord-tenant issues. You want a lawyer very experienced in the type of case you have. The more experienced the lawyer, the better judgment that lawyer has in the field. But that doesn't always mean that the senior lawyer will, or should, handle all aspects of your case. In some firms with several lawyers, a junior lawyer may be assigned to your case while a senior lawyer supervises. This helps keep your costs down while, at the same time, the experienced lawyer has a set of eyes on your case. *Be sure to ask about this.*

## Presence

Does the lawyer have presence and the ability to communicate well? Is he/she diplomatic, professional, and astute? The lawyer will be acting and speaking on your behalf. You want a lawyer who is confident, can think on his/her feet, and can get along with people. The people your lawyer needs to get along with include opposing counsel, the judge, court reporters, office staff, experts, and other consultants that may be required to develop your case. Getting along does not mean agreeing with everyone. It only means that your lawyer is a professional. A lawyer can be professional while vehemently advocating for a client. This skill also includes the ability to negotiate as well as argue on your behalf. Rely heavily on your instincts here when you are interviewing the lawyer at your first meeting.

## Communication

Does the lawyer have the skills to communicate well? Much of a lawyer's work is done in writing. This includes letters, motions filed in court, contracts, documents created to complete transactions, and documents required to comply with government regulations. It will be difficult for you to assess this characteristic before hiring your lawyer. But, if your first written document (an engagement letter, fee agreement, or introductory email) is filled with typographical errors, poor grammar, or weak composition, perhaps that is a sign that the lawyer is a poor communicator.

## Empathy

Does the lawyer understand your situation outside of the legal facts? Although the law will often bring every case down to dollars and cents, a good lawyer will spend some time getting to know you and your objectives. Advocating for a client requires more than just arguing the law. Although you want your lawyer to be strong, a lawyer without emotion and empathy will often fail to tell your story in the best way. The best lawyers are very good at storytelling, and storytelling requires an understanding of the client and client's objectives beyond the legal ramifications.

## Boundaries

Does the lawyer listen to you without over-identifying with your emotional state? Some lawyers have a tendency to assume the same emotional state as their clients. This is not a desirable trait in a lawyer. You need a lawyer because you have a problem that needs to be solved. You may be emotionally involved. One of the values of hiring a lawyer is that the lawyer is detached and objective and can assess your case and see how the case will be viewed by a judge. If the lawyer overly assumes your emotional state, you've lost that objective eye and professional judgment. Recall my lawsuit over my former law partnership. I can say confidently that every client falls short of being entirely objective about his/her own case.

## Time

Does the lawyer have time to take on your case? *This is a big one.* Many clients complain because the lawyer stops communicating with them. Law firms and lawyers are competing for the same work, and sometimes lawyers will take on more than they should. Make sure your lawyer has adequate time for you from the beginning.

## Instinct

What is your gut telling you? There are lots of good lawyers out there. But not every good lawyer is the right lawyer for you. Feel free to comparison shop. You can call or meet a few lawyers and ask questions. Ask each lawyer the questions posed above. Pay attention. What does your intuition tell you while you're talking to the lawyer? Take good notes and spend a little time reflecting on what you learned.

## Red Flags

Red flags are warnings and should be heeded. I have included two red flags, and if either are present, you should run the other way.

A lawyer is prohibited by the rules of ethics to solicit legal business directly from a client. If a lawyer calls you out of the blue and asks you if you need a lawyer and asks for your business, this call may be in violation of the lawyer's duties under the Code of Ethics. Remember that discussion above about trust. If a lawyer is violating the rules of professional conduct to get your business, you are forewarned that the same lawyer may bend or violate other rules when dealing with you as a client.

There are no "guarantees" in the law. Every good lawyer knows that there are strengths and weaknesses in every case, and it's the job of the lawyer to identify what those are. The only thing the lawyer can guarantee is that he/she will put forth his/her best efforts but cannot guarantee a result. *If a lawyer "guarantees" a result in your case, or makes over-the-top promises, there is something wrong.*

## Questions & Conversations

Over the years, I have found that most clients don't ask enough questions. Nearing the end of the interview, I have often asked clients if they had questions or concerns that they haven't expressed. Some clients will ask a question or two, but many will say they don't have any. In response, I usually throw out a couple of questions myself to let the client know that I think there are more questions they should ask. So, as a last resort, you could ask your lawyer this: "What questions have I not asked that you think I should ask."

Remember that you are not only gathering information but interviewing this lawyer to determine if what you hear instills confidence in you so that you can feel comfortable working with this lawyer. Your goal is to find someone you can trust with sensitive information. In order to develop that trust, you need to converse with the lawyer to learn who he/she is and learn what he/she does well. The more you learn, the better you will be able to assess whether you can trust the lawyer and have confidence in him/her.

To help you get started, below is a list of topics to explore with your lawyer. These topics are designed to help you have a conversation with your lawyer, so you have a chance to get to know more about him/her.

1. The lawyer's regular practice and how it involves cases like yours.
2. The lawyer's attitude and philosophy about lawsuits, settlement, alternate dispute resolutions, creative settlements, and alternatives.
3. Ground rules for communication between you, the lawyer, and the lawyer's office.
4. How you can be involved in case preparation that may reduce your costs.
5. The lawyer's office procedure that may impact how you work with the lawyer, the staff, and your role as a client.
6. The lawyer's initial perspective on possible outcomes in your case.
7. Clarity on what you will be charged for and payment policies/options.

Just as you want your potential lawyer to be honest and sincere with you, you must be the same. Remember that you and your lawyer must have mutual trust. As I said, the lawyer is also interviewing you to see if he or she wants you for a client. Your need for information about your lawyer needs to balance with a sincere attempt by both you and the lawyer to get to know each other and learn whether or not you are compatible as a working team.

Lawyers, *good* lawyers, do not feel obligated to take on each and every case. I have had potential clients come into my office with what I would consider very interesting cases—cases in which I would enjoy working because the facts and relevant law were interesting. Yet, as I was interviewing the potential client, I concluded that I did not want to spend time with this potential client. In one case, I concluded that a client was not forthright with me. In another case, the client became hostile simply because I was asking questions. If I feel there will be personality conflicts or trust issues, I will decline the case and refer that client to another lawyer who may be a better fit. Likewise, you should not feel obligated to hire the first lawyer you meet.

If during your interview with your lawyer, you sincerely ask questions to learn more about the lawyer, express any concerns you have and let the lawyer address your concerns, you will be able to determine whether or not you want to work with this person.

## Fee Agreements

When you find a lawyer you can trust, the first thing you must do is enter into a fee agreement.

You and your lawyer should agree on what and how you will pay for services. This agreement should be in writing. Please note: if the lawyer performs services, you will have to pay for them with or without a fee agreement. However, it is in your best interest to have a written agreement. The written fee agreement protects you, so you know what to expect in terms of time and services rendered. No one likes surprises.

The fee agreement should contain some basic information, and before you sign one, you should go over some important questions. Below are some of the questions you can ask.

1. What exactly is your lawyer being hired to do for you?
2. How will the lawyer charge you for time spent on your case?
3. What kinds of activities will be charged to you?
4. Whose activities will be charged to you?

5. Is there anything you can do to help reduce your fees and costs?
6. What are the costs that will be charged to you?
7. Does the lawyer have an estimate for the total charges?*

*Although asking a lawyer for a best estimate of the total charges that might be incurred is fair, you need to understand that these estimates are just numbers that do not include changes in scope or circumstance. If during the representation, a major shift occurs that causes your lawyer to have to do something unanticipated, you will be charged for the extra time spent. Some lawyers don't like giving out estimates because they know so much of what will happen in the future cannot be anticipated.

In most cases, your lawyer will have a pre-printed fee agreement. The pre-printed fee agreements save the lawyer and his staff time. It does not mean that what is in the agreement is set in stone. You should read it carefully and ask questions about anything in the agreement you don't understand or don't particularly like. Again, an honest discussion with your lawyer is the key to having a good start in the relationship.

Because the fee agreement is a contract, it is not uncommon for a lawyer to tell you that you have the right to have a different lawyer look at the contract and advise you. I have done this in a variety of cases, especially for those I have referred to other lawyers because I did not handle the case. It's not a bad idea to go back to the first lawyer you saw, who referred you to this lawyer, to read your contract. Expect to pay for this service, but it should not cost very much.

Whether you choose to read it on your own or hire another lawyer to read the fee agreement, do not sign any fee agreement unless you actually agree with everything in it. You should never sign an agreement you don't agree with.

Below are descriptions of the types of fee agreements that lawyers use and a discussion about the costs associated with legal matters.

## Types of Fee Agreements

Lawyers typically use one of six fee arrangements, depending on the type of case you bring to the lawyer.

**Flat Fee.** A flat fee is a set amount of money to perform a set service. This type of fee is usually used to handle routine matters such a drafting a simple will or preparing other standard documents. In this situation, it is important that you understand what is included in the fee and what is not included. Often costs are not included and can be added to the flat fee.

**Hourly Fee.** This type of arrangement is very common. In an hourly fee, the lawyer charges you a set amount per hour for time spent on your case. If a lawyer charges $400.00 per hour, and he spends 12 minutes (0.2) on your case, you will be charged $80.00. The hourly rate lawyers charge varies significantly depending on how long the lawyer has been practicing, the lawyer's expertise, and even location. Sometimes a lawyer with a higher level of expertise may charge a higher rate, but that lawyer may bring your case to resolution faster. Just be aware that unforeseen circumstances can always cause a case to take longer than expected. And costs are added to the fees.

**Retainer Fee.** This word "retainer" can mean one of two things. First, it can refer to a set amount as a deposit to hire the lawyer so the lawyer is available to take your case. This type of retainer may be refundable or nonrefundable. If the fee agreement states that your retainer is nonrefundable, even if your lawyer does not do the work, you may not receive any portion of the retainer back. It is important that you read the agreement to know whether the retainer is refundable or not. Sometimes lawyers will put a retainer, or deposit, into a trust account as a hedge against future fees but still expect you to pay the bill each month as statements are sent to you. Be sure you understand the expectation and what is required in the agreement before you sign. Wishing it to be a different way is not going to change the written agreement once you sign it. Second, a retainer could mean a fee that's paid to the lawyer to have the lawyer available for a set period of time "on call."

**Contingency Fee.** This type of fee is often used in injury and accident cases. The agreement will state that the attorney's fees will be a percentage of the money you receive when you win the case or settle the case. If you receive no money, there is no fee. However, the costs that have been incurred are still due, and you will have to pay them even if you receive no money in the case.

The agreement should state the percentage clearly. The agreement also should state whether the percentage is calculated on the total amount you receive before or after costs are deducted. Whether costs are taken out before will have a significant impact on how much money is left over for you to pay all the costs. And even if the word "costs" are included, you need to know if the word "costs" includes costs charged by the lawyer or costs you have incurred as a result of your case, such as medical expenses.

## Costs

Almost all fee agreements require you to reimburse the lawyer for "costs," in addition to paying the fees for the lawyer's services. Costs can add up quickly in any case, so it's always best to go through the possible costs and know for what you can be charged.

Here are some typical costs you will see in your list of charges:

1. **Court reporters** take down and transcribe what is said in court and at depositions or any other proceeding in which the parties want an accurate record of everything said. This can include video depositions as well. And in non-criminal matters, this may also include a court reporter who is asked to record what happens in the courtroom.
2. **Court filing fees** are paid for almost every paper filed with the court.
3. **Process servers** serve papers from the lawsuit initiation to subpoenas at trial.

4. **Experts and consultants** typically charge an hourly rate for time spent reviewing your case, examining evidence, and testifying at depositions and in court.
5. **Investigators** are hired to help gather evidence.
6. **Jury fees and mileage** must be paid in civil cases in order to have a jury trial.
7. **Witness fees and mileage and possibly travel expenses** are paid to assure witnesses appear at depositions and in court.
8. **Travel expenses** accrued by the lawyer which are associated with a client's case.

Additional costs that some (but not all) lawyers may charge include:

1. Legal secretarial and other staff time for clerical services including overtime
2. Copying costs (typically a per page charge).
3. Faxing costs
4. Telephone charges for long distance calls
5. Postage, courier, messenger, delivery, and shipping services

You should always discuss costs with the lawyer, so you know in advance what you will or will not have to pay. *I recommend that you have the lawyer list what you will be paying for in the fee agreement and state that no other costs will be charged to you.*

## Trust Accounts

Almost every lawyer today has a Client Trust Account. This is an account that contains money that does not belong to the lawyer. The funds in the account belong to clients. If a case is settled, the settlement proceeds can go into the trust account. If you give your lawyer deposit money toward fees, the money still belongs to you and belongs in the trust account until it is earned. Lawyers keep all clients' money in one bank account but must have a system that shows how much money belongs to which client.

These accounts must be balanced every month. Ledgers in some format must have a list of clients and how much money belongs to each client. The money cannot be distributed without the client's knowledge. Unless the lawyer has an agreement with the client and has earned the money, the lawyer cannot take any of the money. If you have money in a lawyer's trust account, you should receive an accounting every month, so you can see how much is in there.

The ethics rules have very strict and special guidelines that govern these trust accounts.

∽

This chapter emphasized the need to find a good lawyer and provided you with guidance on how to find your good lawyer. Once you've found your good lawyer, you need to carefully read and sign a fee agreement. Be mindful in selecting your lawyer and remember that mutual trust is essential to your lawyer-client relationship.

# IV. Things to Know about the Legal System

*"Knowledge is power."*

Francis Bacon

Lawyers understand that by the time you seek their help, typically, you are frustrated. You have a problem, and you want it solved—yesterday. We get that. Lawyers would very much like to pull out a magic wand and fix everything for you. Unfortunately, lawyers aren't magicians, and the law does not work so quickly. Lawyering is a slow, tedious job, but every lawyer understands your plight.

As a result of this frustration (which is normal), clients sometimes act in ways that increase the burden *which in turn can cost more money, increase stress and, in subtle ways, weaken your case.* Everything in this section is designed to help you reduce stress and cost and work with your lawyer to put your best case forward.

The categories used here are not accepted, universal classifications; rather, they are used to break up the information in a sensible way that will make it easier to digest.

# Why Do Lawsuits Take So Long?

## *"The Wheels of Justice Turn Slowly"*

The legal system has always been slow, and it is not likely to speed up in the foreseeable future. Below, I have covered a number of topics to inform you of inner workings of the law to mitigate some frustration. When dealing with courts, opposing lawyers, witnesses, and calendars, many factors influence the speed with which anything can happen. Be aware of as much of this as possible; set up reasonable expectations; save yourself much stress fretting over things you and your lawyer cannot control.

## Court System

Each day, more and more lawsuits are filed, clogging further an already congested court system. Many judges have hundreds of cases they must review. Add state and county budgetary restraints, and the courthouse staff is reduced, making more work for less staff, and creating more backlog of processing documents. In some courts, when you file a piece of paper, it may take weeks before it actually physically reaches a file. Electronic docketing and scanning systems might get the paper into the court's system in several days (rather than weeks), but it will not be instantaneous.

In fact, lawyers are frustrated that the legal system moves so slowly. They are frustrated when they can't get a hearing for six months. They are frustrated when it takes a long time for a judge to issue a decision. They are frustrated when they have to sit and wait for their matters to be heard.

Judges are equally frustrated with the ever increasing congestion of the legal system. Most judges spent considerable time during the day managing cases rather than deliberating on the points of law and intricate questions raised in each case. Most judges have to take home files and briefs in order to deal with the cases themselves. Most judges have lawyers as research clerks, but even the research clerks are overwhelmed with cases. Judges prefer to get their decisions out quickly, but backlog interferes with the speed with which judges can get to cases. Add trials to the workload when judges are locked into listening to one case for several days, or several weeks, and the backlog in other cases increases. Court clerks have to limit the number of cases on a particular hearing calendar, which are almost always full, to prevent those hearings from running all day.

However there are ways we lawyers can navigate the system more effectively. One morning, I left my office at 8:45 for court to argue a motion set for a 9:00 a.m. calendar. When I arrived at the courthouse, I looked at the calendar, which was several pages posted on the wall outside the court room. I was on a calendar of 45 cases, mine listed in the high 30s. This meant I probably would be sitting in this courtroom for the entire morning before my case was called. Fortunately, I knew this judge always asked lawyers if they had a case in which they had said everything that needed to be said in their motion papers. He invited those *prepared* lawyers to submit on the papers, waive argument, and leave. I found opposing counsel, and he agreed to submit early on the papers. (I also strongly felt that we couldn't lose the motion.) When the calendar was called and the judge invited submissions, I was the first to stand and submit. I was back in my office by 9:15 a.m. I was happy that this entire motion process took only half hour, rather than sitting and waiting in a courtroom for two to three hours. I could move on to something else more productive. (And yes, we won the motion.)

**Your good lawyer wants you to know** that he/she is just as frustrated as you are with the slow speed of the legal system and does not like spending time waiting for things to happen.

## Court Calendars

Contrary to what you see in movies and television shows, lawyers do not get matters before a judge on the same day; trials are not set a week after you meet with the lawyer. Hardly anything is considered an "emergency" in the legal system.

When matters are set on a court calendar, sometimes a matter has to be continued for a variety of reasons. Rather than putting off the matter a couple of days, the judge will continue it 30 days. This not only allows for ample time to allow the parties to get things done, but the court's calendar likely has no room. Here's a rule of thumb we use in our office: if it might take us one day to accomplish the task, it's a 30-day continuance; if it takes two to four days to accomplish, it's a 60-day continuance. If it takes more than four days to accomplish, figure on a 90-day continuance. We go to court asking for less time, but this timetable is realistic and can help manage expectations.

**Your good lawyer wants you to know** that he/she tries very hard to have your cases set as soon as possible and to have continuances for shorter periods of time, but there are many factors out of your lawyer's control involved in setting court dates.

## Multiple Calendars

In every lawsuit, outside of the courtroom, there are many instances when the lawyers from both sides must coordinate their calendars to take depositions, set up mediations, arbitrations, and even trials. All of these situations involve other persons who may include you, the other side, witnesses, expert witnesses, and court reporters. When scheduling any of these events, your lawyer has to find a date that works for everyone involved. Coordinating all these calendars takes time. Once a date is set, if something were to happen to any of the players, it has to be reset. In a typical lawsuit, having to postpone events and resetting dates is common practice.

**Your good lawyer wants you to know** that he/she is always trying to find the earliest date that works for everyone who has to be present at each event.

## Time

Lawyers spend a good deal of time to prepare documents. With electronic research capabilities, lawyers can research more information in less time, but the time spent on strategy and writing is not reduced. Documents that are eventually filed with the courts are often revised numerous times before suitable for filing. The documents we submit to the court are called *briefs*. Although we lawyers often joke that our briefs are far from "brief," good lawyers work hard to say what they need to say succinctly. This takes time.

> *"I didn't have time to write a short letter, so I wrote a long one instead."*
>
> Mark Twain

In addition to wanting to be brief, in most cases, the law and the courts have imposed page limitations to the documents lawyers file. Page limitations force lawyers to edit briefs. We write, re-write, and edit court papers in order to convey complex information, to be clear and to the point, and yet complete. These constraints help the judges so that they do not have to read massive amounts in each case. Imagine a judge faced with 40+ cases in one hearing calendar. Even with a typical 15-page limitation (for each side, assuming there are only two sides), the judge has over 1200 pages to read for one hearing calendar.

Your lawyer spends considerable time identifying key facts, excluding information that will not impact the outcome, culling statutes and often multiple cases to make the best argument on your behalf. The opposing side is the doing the same (hopefully). In our office, when we receive papers from the opposing lawyer that have been well-edited, we are relieved because it makes our jobs a little easier. When we receive papers from a lawyer who is less diligent, our job is made much harder because we have to figure out what the other side is really trying to say, so we can effectively respond (a reason to hope that the other side has a good lawyer, too).

By the time you, the client, receive the end product, the 15 pages has been edited and re-edited significantly. If you look only at the 15 pages, you might wonder why your cost for this document is $5,000. Now you know why.

**Your good lawyer wants you to know** that he/she takes great pride in doing the best work possible to advance your cause, but this takes time.

## Technology

Although courts are trying to automate systems to make it more efficient, the legal system lags behind technologically.

Despite online filing, automated docketing systems, and telephonic appearances, the legal system requires lawyers to argue and judges to consider. So long as more and more lawsuits are filed each day, technology cannot eliminate the congestion and the time it takes for every lawyer and every judge to read the thousands of pages of papers filed in one lawsuit. The use of *alternate dispute resolution* (discussed later) is likely the one factor that can save you and everyone in the system.

**Your good lawyer wants you to know** that he/she understands your desire to resolve your legal case quickly and efficiently at the lowest cost possible. Many delays that occur are indicative of a sluggish system.

∽

## Show Me | Show Me | Show Me

In every lawsuit, three threads present difficulty for clients. In this section, I explain and clarify why you need to understand the three components below. It seems that no matter how sophisticated the client—business or individual—these three areas are sources for client frustration.

## Show Me the Money

The number one reality check every client needs to have early on in a lawsuit, by and large, is that lawsuits are motivated by monetary outcomes. Yes, there are those rare exceptions when something else might matter. If you have one of those rare cases, trust me, your lawyer will tell you. The legal system is not designed to illicit an apology, prove you are right, agree with you, be nice to you, force someone to admit being wrong or feel bad for getting away with something. The legal system is about arriving at a satisfactory payoff. Some clients understand this because the money is their goal from the beginning. Some clients have difficulty with this because when the lawsuit begins, although monetary retribution is the desired outcome, there may be a whole lot more going on.

Your lawyer understands that there are strong emotions around your case. Sometimes a client hires a lawyer because *it's about the principle* and claims the money is irrelevant. Some simply want an apology. Others will say that the person "in the wrong" just can't be allowed to "get away with it." If an apology is all the client is looking for, then this needs to be addressed early on before lawsuits are filed and before anyone has spent considerable dollars defending their positions. The legal system cannot provide you anything more than money. Almost every client who began on "principle" winds up concerned about money whether coming in or going out. Now go back up and read the first paragraph of this section again. Like it or not, the money always matters.

Here's an example of someone using the court for the wrong reason. A woman, called Sue, owned a condominium. She leased it to another woman named Mary for a year. At the end of the year, Mary was preparing to move out. Sue went to the condo and did a walk-through; it was filthy and had a lot of damage. Sue took photos and made an extensive list of the damage. In the meantime, Mary managed to fix everything before she moved out. When Sue got the keys and did a second walk-through, the condo was in good shape. This time Mary took photographs. Sue was so upset; she filed a lawsuit anyway. Her condo was one of the most precious things in her life. I was sitting as the judge and as Sue presented her case in court, she began crying. There was no doubt that Sue was genuinely upset about what she had seen and after seeing the photos. I understood why she felt how she felt. Unfortunately, the condo was ultimately left in good condition, and therefore no cleaning or repairs were necessary. Sue did not want money; she wanted Mary to apologize and say that how she treated Sue's unit was wrong. She felt "people shouldn't get away with treating other people's property so poorly." But unless Mary voluntarily apologized, there was nothing I could do to give Sue what she wanted.

This is an extreme example over a small matter, but it illustrates the point. The sooner you realize the court system is about recovering money, the easier it is to make decisions about your case.

One of our business clients is a sole entrepreneur who has the money to fight if he wants to. Sometimes he gets angry and wants to sue. Lawyers will check with the opposing side to see if a problem can be solved before filing a lawsuit. In so doing, we have avoided many lawsuits with this client by just getting the other side to apologize. Once the other side apologized, our client did not care about the monetary loss anymore, and he moved on. It was much easier to get an apology before legal action was taken. If these apologies had not come through, and a lawsuit had been filed, the focus would turn to money, and only money.

The above example does not mean you don't share your concerns with your lawyer. Your lawyer needs to know everything that is motivating you so that your concerns can be addressed. Knowing all of your concerns can help your lawyer have an eye open to alternative ways to solve your problem.

But bear in mind that you did not hire your lawyer to deal with how you have been hurt emotionally. Yes we are sympathetic—we get it. However, therapists and friends are a lot cheaper than your lawyer. Your lawyer wants to get you through the legal issue, so you can move on with your life. Trust that your lawyer will keep you on track. Do not take offense when your lawyer shortens the time spent on how upset you are feeling and brings you back to the only available solution: money.

**Your good lawyer wants you to know** that when he/she keeps bringing you back to the discussion of money, it is because this is the end game of every lawsuit, not because he/she doesn't understand how you feel.

## Show Me the Facts

In preparing for this section in the book, I called a lawyer friend of mine and asked him if he had ever heard a client say, "Oh, I didn't think that was important." He laughed immediately and responded, "Let me count the ways." Now go ask your lawyer if any client has ever said that to him/her. I bet that they would have a similar reaction. The facts of a case are what drive everything.

All the law in the world has limited value in the absence of facts. Lawyers need to know all the facts up front. The lawyer can't help you unless you disclose all the facts, including the ones you don't like and including the ones you think are not true, or important. But most clients don't tell the lawyer everything in the beginning. Lawyers really don't like to be blindsided by client omission simply because the client did not like the fact (or perhaps forgot). This is one of the reasons why the lawyer you hire asks you many probing questions, and may ask the same questions over again later. You might think that the lawyer does not believe you but the lawyer is just trying to collect information and jog your memory to assure all the facts are revealed. From experience, your lawyer knows that clients often omit facts. Irrespective of the reasons, the omitted facts can be crucial. Leaving it out can cost you considerable expense and stress and interfere with your lawyer's ability to help you.

Almost every judge in trial courts, appellate courts and supreme courts in every state and in federal courts, up to the United States Supreme Court, has written (repeatedly) that the law is only as good as the facts in the case. Lawyers are always trying to find decided cases that have facts similar to your facts. But if the lawyer has only part of the facts, all that research is going to have meaningless results.

In our office, we ask our clients, "What's the other side saying about this?" Our client often knows precisely what the other side is saying. Even though the client will preface the report by disclaiming any truth to the facts (which is fine), at least we get the facts and the other side's story.

We understand that when a lawyer is looking for holes in your case, it may feel as if your lawyer is not on your side. I've heard clients complain that their lawyer isn't "working for them," or doesn't "believe in them." Trust me, you *want* your lawyer to be looking for holes in your case so that the holes, if any, can be patched up if possible. If you were on a ship, you'd want your captain more concerned with the holes in the hull, than the perfect polish on the deck railing.

I have heard clients complain that their lawyer is not advocating for them; the lawyer keeps digging and digging, question after question, and the client often feels as if the lawyer is being offensive and aggressive. In fact the lawyer is "challenging" you to uncover every aspect of your situation. Better to have your lawyer do the digging and be prepared for eventualities, than be surprised when someone else does even more digging and surprises you and your lawyer.

Eventually, most facts do get revealed. If there are any facts that may harm your position, you can assume the other side is gathering those facts to be used against you. If those facts come out later, all the work your lawyer has done to that point has to be shelved and more work is needed. That work is often the time consuming work of research and analysis. By keeping secrets, or by being less than diligent in conveying the facts, you just increased your lawyer's time and your fees.

If you are holding facts back, you have potentially increased your stress levels as well. There is no guarantee that telling your lawyer all the facts, especially the negative ones, will help resolve all your problems the way you want. But not telling your lawyer is causing you to spend wasted energy keeping a secret which could likely backfire on you. Tell your lawyer and let your lawyer worry about how to work with the facts.

**Your good lawyer wants you to know** that your good facts are strong and that's the easy part; revealing and working with the not-so-good-facts is the hard part, and that's what you are paying your lawyer to deal with.

## Show Me the Evidence

At first blush, "Show Me the Evidence" may seem the same as the last section "Show Me the Facts." But evidence and facts are not the same. Understanding the difference will help you understand the work your lawyer does.

Knowing the **facts** helps your lawyer figure out what **evidence** must be gathered. Gathering evidence is finding the source that can be used in court to prove your facts. You may need to dig up the original deed. You may need to get the address of a witness who told you something. Your lawyer is first asking you to *show him/her the facts*. Once you get to the court, the judge is expecting you to *show him/her the evidence*.

For instance, our client tells us that the other side is lying. The other side might very well be lying. But if I go to court and say, "Objection! The witness is lying," the judge will look at me crossly and tell me to sit down. If the witness is saying that you didn't pay the rent for the past six months, and you say you did pay the rent, those are **facts**. Now, you need to bring me the **evidence** that proves you paid the rent such as a cancelled check.

When your lawyer is looking for the evidence, your lawyer is not working against you. Your lawyer is doing what must be done in order to prepare your case for a judge or jury.

**Your good lawyer wants you to know** that you do not have to decide in advance what is fact or evidence; that's the lawyer's job. Bring it *all* in; but, *all* must come to your lawyer.

# Professionalism

*"Whoever is careless with the truth in small matters cannot be trusted with important matters."*

Albert Einstein

### Lawyer's Reputation in Court

Your lawyer has spent considerable time and energy building a reputation of *trust* with the court, court staff, and members of the legal community. This reputation helps you. The reputation stems from professionalism, courtesy, and integrity.

A lawyer's reputation is built by consistently being honest and ethical in presenting the facts of a cases. Every judge knows that lawyers must zealously advocate for their clients. But good lawyers don't need to "fudge" facts or falsely accuse. Your lawyer has a naturally strategic mind—always calculating to determine the best way to present your case within ethical bounds.

Judges talk. Clerks talk. Bailiffs talk. Research clerks talk. They will all form opinions about which lawyers are trustworthy. Your lawyer has judiciously established his/her integrity through hundreds of cases before helping you. One time, I went to the Court of Appeal clerk's office to deliver some documents. The head clerk just happened to be there, and he was taking my papers. As we were chatting, he turned to me and asked me if I was involved in a particular case. I wasn't and responded "No." He shook his head and stated, "One of the clerks said you had called on that case and was really rude to her. I told her it couldn't have been you. I knew she was mistaken about the name of the lawyer." *Whew!* I was relieved. Had I not had the reputation in advance of being courteous to the courthouse staff, the head clerk may not even have presented me with the question. My reputation saved my reputation.

Lawyers are human. They slip up at times. But if that lawyer has a good reputation with the court, an occasional negative incident can be overlooked, forgiven, and fixed.

Another time, I missed a court appearance. I, as with all lawyers, have redundant calendaring systems to prevent precisely this type of event from happening. But it did happen. I realized my error about an hour after the scheduled court appearance. I ran to the courthouse, hoping that today's calendar was long with my case near the end and perhaps I could still make it. That was not the case. I showed up; the courtroom was empty. The judge was already in his chambers. The door to his clerk's office was open. I poked my head in. She smiled and said, "We missed you this morning." I smiled back and said, "I just messed up and missed it. I'm so sorry." Her response was, "Oh, don't worry. The judge commented you must be proud of your papers and took your motion under submission." Later I learned that the court clerk told the judge that I had come by and told her that I had just missed the hearing by mistake. I didn't make up some excuse (dog ate my briefcase or there was traffic). My reputation stood for me. That judge knew that he could trust me; he could trust what I say in court; he could trust what

I say and argue in my court papers. (Incidentally, the judge ruled in my client's favor on the motion.)

Little things that the lawyer does in the community have big consequences. It is often those seemingly little things that reveal one's true character.

**Your good lawyer wants you to know** that his/her trustworthy reputation with the court works in your favor at all times.

## Lawyer's Reputation in the Community

Good lawyers work at being cordial with other lawyers. Lawyers' relationships are not much different from professional sports figures who demonstrate good sportsmanship. When on the field, the players battle fiercely. When the game is over, they shake hands, and congratulate each other on a game well-played.

Clients are often taken aback when they see their lawyer being friendly with the opposing side's lawyer and wonder why their lawyer is "fraternizing with the enemy." Your lawyer is not fraternizing; your lawyer is being cordial, civil, and respectful because that is how good lawyers conduct themselves. You need to know that we lawyers are always "on," always watchful and carefully listening for anything that might be to your advantage, and the opposing lawyer is doing the same. Not having on full battle dress or sword drawn does not mean your lawyer isn't working your case.

Clients may feel that their lawyer should exhibit the same level of passion that he/she feels when the lawyer goes to court or to a meeting with opposing counsel. You do not want your lawyer adopting your level of emotion when working on your case or when encountering opposing counsel or any member of the legal community. A benefit to hiring a lawyer is his/her objectivity when you are emotionally involved. Your emotional involvement, although quite natural and understandable, interferes with good judgment and sound actions. Your lawyer's "objectivity" is your safety net—the voice of reason which allows your lawyer to be calculating.

Mutual cooperation between lawyers is essential. You don't want your lawyer having to go to court every time something is needed. Likewise, your good lawyer is not going to make the other lawyer run to court every time something is needed, especially when your lawyer knows the judge will grant the request anyway. Sadly, some lawyers take advantage of the situation.

For example when a continuance is requested, whether from a deadline to file papers or to move a hearing date, most deadlines are not "deadly," and judges are generous about allowing extra time. Continuances are part of the process. Whether your lawyer is asking for (or granting) a continuance, this is not something to fret over. If the other side repeatedly asks for continuances that appear unnecessary, your lawyer can, and will, stop cooperating.

There are many instances when a simple agreement between the lawyers can eliminate the need to go to the judge for something the judge is likely to grant anyway. When to agree, or not agree, is a judgment call that you need to let your lawyer make. Again, everything your lawyer does, every agreement your lawyer makes with the other side is calculated to better represent you.

**Your good lawyer wants you to know** that courtesy and cooperation between lawyers helps him/her do a better job for you and can save you a great deal of money, time, and stress.

## Case Resolution

Have you ever been on jury duty and learned the night before that you didn't have to report? Many cases can be set for trial on the day you were supposed to report as a juror, but most, if not all, of those cases may have settled the day before. Resolving cases before they ever get to trial is common practice.

Today courts are pushing to get cases settled, in part, to relieve the congestion. Additionally, the courts recognize that most cases can, and should, settle.

The court *will* send you to a settlement conference and alternate dispute resolution (mediation or arbitration) whether you want to or not.

## Settlement

In business transactions, settlement is a way of life. Business professionals are involved in negotiations almost daily. Every minute spent in litigation or in trial is time and money lost. Time spent in litigation and at trial is just bad for business, yet sometimes it can't be avoided.

As previously mentioned, since lawsuits are all about money, whether it involves you or your business, the lawsuit is about business decision-making. Treat it like a business. Every minute and every dollar you spend trying to get to trial is bad business. Let your lawyer help resolve your dispute faster and always consider settlement as an option.

At some point in every decision, we all have to do a risk-cost-benefit analysis. In the business world, this is commonplace. It does not make sense to spend $10.00 to go after $9.00. Most people see the logic of this concept. But, if you have to spend $9.00 to go after $10.00 gaining only $1.00, do you go for that? In that situation, you have to ask if the time spent and stress you experience is worth the $1.00 gain. Settling does not mean folding. It means being reasonable, ready to take a little less or pay a little more. It's a compromise. Fortunately, you have a *good lawyer* now on your side to advise you and assure that your settlement will be satisfactory.

One of the major benefits to settling is having control over the outcome of your case. You can be creative when settling. Sometimes you can even get that apology you wanted. You can give up things that do not matter to you but which may matter a great deal to the other side. Although you may not be 100% happy with the result, you can live with it. Because a settlement involves an agreement between both sides, you can leave shaking hands, even if you are not going to be best friends afterwards. This is something lawyers often see.

The flip side to settling is doing battle to the end. This means going to trial. Just know that a trial is a gamble, no matter how good you think your case is or how good your lawyer is. You never know how a judge or jury will respond. You don't even know in advance if the judge or jury will believe you, even if you are telling the whole truth and nothing but the truth! Sometimes trial is inevitable, yet it always remains a gamble.

When discussing a settlement, in addition to the strengths and weaknesses of your case and the other side's case, you should consider the practical aspects of what would happen if you went to trial and won. Let's assume you win everything you want. Then what?

Is the other side likely to appeal? An **appeal** is challenging the result in the next higher court. For practical purposes, consider the appeal a whole new lawsuit. An appeal has different rules than litigation and trial, and can take another year or two. Appeals are expensive. Often a losing side will file the appeal just to create leverage in an attempt to force another settlement discussion. The cost and time for appeal can and will be an added burden.

If the other side does not appeal, what are the chances they will just write you a check? Are you going to have trouble collecting your award? Is there a chance the other side might file bankruptcy?

Trust that your lawyer understands your case and the risk of success at trial and the possibilities of events after trial. Listen to your lawyer's advice regarding settlement. When you are at a settlement table, it is a business transaction, not an emotional one.

**Your good lawyer wants you to know** that even in a settlement negotiation, he/she is weighing all the positive points in your case to leverage the best result for you. Your lawyer considers the big picture, which includes what is happening now and what may transpire in the future.

## Early Settlement and ADR

In many contract cases, the contract requires the parties to try **Alternative Dispute Resolution (ADR)**, such as mediation or arbitration, before a lawsuit may be filed. **Mediation** is settlement. Mediation does not resolve a case until and unless all the parties agree. In mediation you have control over the outcome. **Arbitration** is an informal trial where both sides present their case and the arbitrator will eventually make a decision. In arbitration, you do not have control over the outcome, but the process is faster, less formal and often cheaper than going to trial.

In many cases, when you signed the contract, you agreed to mandatory ADR before filing a lawsuit. Ignoring these provisions in a contract can cause you to lose legal rights if you jump ahead and file a lawsuit. Even before these ADR provisions were added to contracts, most lawyers would try to settle cases cooperatively before filing the lawsuits. This is because once a lawsuit is filed, people tend to dig in their heels making settlement more difficult.

Utilizing ADR before filing a lawsuit can be beneficial. It is a valuable tool in resolving disputes. Today, highly experienced mediators and arbitrators are available to help. Many are retired judges and may have valuable insight into how a judge will view your case. They also have insight into how juries respond to a variety of issues and evidence. Although ADR isn't necessarily cheap, it is certainly less expensive and faster than going to trial.

You do not have to wait until the eve of trial when the judge sends you to a settlement conference to consider and explore ADR/settlement. Some of the most creative settlements have come from ADR.

**Your good lawyer wants you to know** that he/she is always looking at alternate means to resolve your case short of going to trial in order to save you money and stress.

## Our Case is a Slam Dunk!

An experienced lawyer once said to me, "I only take winning cases to trial. I settle everything else." That sounded like good advice to me. After all, why would you take a bad case to trial knowing you were going to lose? But if lawyers only took winning cases to trial, then an equal number of lawyers were taking bad cases to trial (the side that loses). If *all* lawyers only took winning cases to trial, there would never be any trials. And there's the key.

What defines a good case, bad case, or mediocre case? Every case has two sides. In *most* cases, there are unknowns on both sides. Rarely does a lawyer have a case in which he/she can say, "This is a slam dunk. We are going to win this no matter what happens." In nearly 30 years of practice, I had one of those rare cases, but it never went to trial.

Here's my example of the one slam dunk case. A client came to me with a promissory note secured by a deed of trust against his home. The note required the client to pay the loan amount along with 21% interest that had accrued for five years. The client didn't have enough to pay it all but could pay the loan and some interest. My first reaction was that the interest was usurious. In other words, it was so high it was against the law. But there are many exceptions to the usury law. First, I had to determine if any exceptions applied. Eventually, I took a deposition of the "lender" and asked questions about every exception to find out if any applied. The lender revealed that no exception applied. Despite having the evidence that my case was a "slam dunk winner," the lender would not settle. But, instead of going to trial, I used a motion procedure to show the court that my client would win, no matter what. We won through the motion procedure less than six months after we started without the time and expense of trial.

If it's truly a slam dunk, you don't need to go to trial. There are other ways to resolve the case without the time and expense of trial. Even if you think it's almost a slam dunk, these procedures are in place to help resolve cases short of trial.

**Your good lawyer wants you to know** that he/she is aware of procedures that exist to bring your case to resolution without a trial and will use them when appropriate.

~

## How Much Do We Get or Have to Pay?

In every lawsuit, the ultimate question that every client asks is, "How much money will I receive [or have to pay]?" Figuring how much a litigant may receive (or pay) can be very complicated. The law has different "measures" to calculate how much can be recovered for different kinds of cases. The law also defines what types of damages can be recovered for different kinds of cases. **Contract damages** tend to be very black and white and do not allow for punishing people. Extremely horrific situations may trigger **punitive damages** which is a form of civil punishment. Between these extremes, there exists a multitude of ways the law calculates how much you might receive or how much you might have to pay. Below I have discussed the two extreme examples because these examples tend to be the most misunderstood by clients when they first encounter the legal system.

### Punitive Damages

Here is a topic that often throws people for a loop. Everyone has heard about punitive damages—the windfall—the get-rich-quick award.

You may be familiar with one of the most famous cases in which a jury awarded punitive damages: The McDonalds Coffee Case. In that case, Ms. Liebeck sued McDonalds because she placed a cup of their coffee between her legs and drove away. The coffee spilled and scalded her; sadly, she suffered third-degree burns. Ms. Liebeck spent eight days in the hospital, underwent skin grafting, and endured two years of medical treatments. The jury awarded Ms. Liebeck $160,000 for medical expenses and $2.7 million in punitive damages. The case did not end there. The trial judge actually reduced the total damages to $640,000, and McDonalds appealed. The parties ended up settling for a confidential amount before the appeal was decided.

The main point here is that the jury awarded $2.7 million in punitive damages. When most people hear about this case, they react with astonishment that the case ever went to trial. After all, who would expect a paper cup full of fresh, hot coffee not to spill when set between one's knees while driving? Nevertheless, this case made it to a jury trial. Setting aside for the moment who was responsible for the injury, let's look at what happened to Ms. Liebeck. She suffered third-degree burns, spent eight days in the hospital, underwent painful skin grafting, and two years of medical treatment. She suffered immensely. Unless you have experienced that kind of pain, and the person/business you are suing has been grossly negligent, punitive damages are not likely to be awarded. In business-type cases, rarely are punitive damages even requested, must less awarded. Punitive damages are most common in intentional physical injury cases.

I'm not suggesting you avoid discussing punitive damages. Feel free to ask. The lawyer will bluntly tell you if your case is eligible for punitive damages. If your case warrants requesting them, your lawyer will definitely ask for them. Just because punitive damages are not available, does not mean you have a weak case. Accept it and move on. The law is set up to "measure" your precise monetary loss. No more, no less. But do yourself a favor; don't bank on punitive damages as a windfall to change your life.

**Your good lawyer wants you to know**, if your case involves the type of facts and claims that can justify an award of punitive damages, he/she will ask for them. But asking for them is not a guarantee that a judge or jury will award them. Punitive damages cases are rare. Awards of large punitive damage cases happen to be highly publicized so you hear about almost all of them, while you rarely hear about the thousands of other cases in which none was awarded.

## Contract Damages

Again, many legal problems result from someone breaking a contract. This book is not the place to go into detail about how contract damages are calculated, or what is included in the myriad of situations for which you may be entitled to damages. But it is important to know that damage calculations are solely determined by the exact amount of economic loss that you can **a)** prove you actually suffered and **b)** that is needed to "make you whole."

Often clients are more upset when someone breaks a contract without good reason than if someone breaks a contract with good reason. The law does not distinguish between good and bad reasons. Motivation is irrelevant.

To illustrate, let's say the Smiths signed a contract to buy your house for $625,000 cash, even though the appraisal came in at $600,000. There is no loan contingency. Right before close of escrow, the Smiths call you in a panic. Mrs. Smith was recently diagnosed with cancer, and the money they were going to use to pay you is going towards medical bills. If they don't buy your house, you'll have to put the house back on the market for $600,000, and you will lose $25,000.

Now, let's say Bob Jones, a wealthy business man, signed the contract instead. Just before the close of escrow, Bob calls you and tells you that he found a better deal. Down the street, there's a house listed for $500,000 that's worth $1 million, and he's breaking your contract. He tells you he doesn't care if you sue him; in fact, he doesn't really like you and is glad you are losing money. He can pay your $25,000 any time, or not.

The money you would be entitled to in both cases is the same: $25,000. It doesn't matter that you might feel sympathetic toward the Smiths and be willing to walk away from $25,000; yet, you are angry with Bob and want to make him suffer by getting more money from him.

Beyond being realistic about amounts legally available, clients sometimes feel that their lawyer isn't doing the most for them when the lawyer is not asserting in court (or with the other party's lawyer) how "bad" that person is. As the injured party, it is almost irresistible to go on about the other party. Your lawyer is going to put a buffer on those feelings because that is in your best interest.

In trial, your lawyer will want the judge or jury to know that the other fellow is a "bad guy." However, he will accomplish that by demonstrating it, not by ranting and raving. Your lawyer will do this in order to damage the other fellow's credibility in court, but it will not change the amount of damages you are entitled to receive.

**Your good lawyer wants you to know** that he/she understands the other party may be a "bad" guy; but he/she will nonetheless focus you on the measure of damages available and what you can or cannot prove with the evidence.

## Other Damages

Besides contract and punitive damages, there are other *measures* of damages for other wrongs that can occur in the legal setting and depending on the type of case involved, the law may have unique methods for calculating damages. This book is not the place to list every type of injury and every type of measure of damages that exist. I included contract and punitive damages because they seem to be the more common types of damages that clients know about. But know that there are many ways to calculate damages. It all depends on the precise facts of your case and the precise law that applies. Again, *it depends*.

**Your good lawyer wants you to know** that he/she waits to know all your facts and researches which laws may apply before he/she can determine precisely how damages may be calculated in your case.

## Other Things to Consider

This section could be called the "reality check" because it involves several areas in which clients often have false impressions of the legal system and how it works. Sometimes these misunderstandings are the result of watching TV and movie dramas or just feeling that your rights need more vindication than is available in the legal system.

### Leave Drama for TV & Movies

It may sound odd, but leave the acting to TV & the movies, *please*.

Sometimes a client takes on "roles" that he/she believes may be more effective in court or in interacting with the other side. Let your lawyer be your courtroom coach who decides what is most effective. You do not need to add anything to the mix.

One of the roles of a judge is to be discerning. When I'm sitting as a judge, I certainly evaluate the participants. When one side is testifying, the other party or other lawyer may snicker, roll eyes, or make some other gesture of disbelief. I tend to believe that these gestures are for the benefit of the court in an attempt to covertly send a message that the other side is untrustworthy or unreasonable. I can tell you that these expressions are not only distracting; they are also unconvincing.

I can guarantee that when anyone in court, whether it be a client, a witness or even the lawyer, starts "acting out" in reaction to what someone else is saying, it decidedly takes away from the actor's own credibility.

Before going to any meeting with the opposition, whether it be negotiations, a deposition, arbitration, mediation, a settlement conference, a court hearing, or trial, at some point, your lawyer will tell you to be neutral. Do not makes faces, gestures, sounds, or react to anything anyone else says or does. (The exception is if someone genuinely makes you cry. Go ahead and cry but do so discreetly.)

By remaining neutral and by quietly taking notes, you increase your credibility and empower your lawyer. When you react, you've created yet another thing your lawyer has to deal with. This makes you and your situation more vulnerable.

Remember, your lawyer has carefully considered how to present your case. When, and if, your lawyer decides to add drama to your case, it is not spontaneous; it's calculated. Don't sabotage what your lawyer has spent hours, days, sometimes weeks and months, preparing by letting your emotions get the better of you.

**Your good lawyer wants you to know** if there is to be any drama at all, please leave it to him/her to plan and stage it, so that drama is never an accident.

## The Law is Wrong!

Sometimes clients are told what the law is and how it applies, and it just doesn't seem right or fair. The client's reaction is, "The law is just wrong!" And the client wants the lawyer to do something about it.

The lawyer's job is to fashion arguments within the existing law to obtain the best results for the client. Lawyers don't make the law. They just use and uphold the law. If you don't like the law and want to change it, you will have to head for the State Capitol and speak to someone in the Legislature. Yelling at your lawyer is not going to help you or change the law.

Remember that "slam dunk" case I mentioned earlier? The opponent, the lender, who charged my client usurious interest, was not a bad person. In fact, the lender was an elderly gentleman who had been in the banking business for many years and had retired a few years back. He had experience with lenders charging high interest rates on a variety of loans that were secured by real property. When he sold the property and lent the money to my client, he did so to assist my client to buy the property. My client was happy with the purchase. But the lender was not a bank; therefore, he was not authorized to charge more than 10% interest at the time. He was not a bad man intending to injure my client. He simply made an innocent mistake. Imagine how he must have felt when he learned that because of this mistake with the interest rate, he lost all of his interest on the loan! He was going to get his principal back but without any interest. To him, this didn't seem fair. But the law is the law.

This point seems simple and self-evident. Nonetheless, I can almost guarantee that you will forget it when your lawyer gives you legal answers or opinions that are not the answers or opinions you want to hear. I have good clients with whom I have worked for many years and who fully trust and rely on me. Yet, on occasion, when I say, "No, George, you can't do that because the law says something else," I see that momentary hesitation. I see the look that says, "The law is wrong. The whole system is wrong, and you are part of it. I thought you were on my side." Again, I can almost guarantee that you won't be able to avoid such reactions from time to time. But maybe now you will recognize it when it happens, reflect on it, and return to the only reality your lawyer can deal with sooner, so you can make the practical decisions and move forward.

**Your good lawyer wants you to know** he/she doesn't like the unfavorable law any more than you do.

## Fault v. Injury

In every lawsuit, there are two parts that have to be proven separately. One is **fault** and the other is **injury.**

Sometimes a client has suffered a loss or *injury*. In order to recover for this injury, the client wants the other side to pay for the injury. However, before the other side is required to pay anything, the other side's *fault* must be proven. Without legally recognized fault, the law will not make the other side pay anything.

I recently sat as a judge on a construction case. The owner of the property had suffered significant water damage to his home which caused massive mold to grow in and underneath the bathroom and kitchen area. He had hired professionals to inspect and remove the mold. He sued a contractor who had been making various repairs to the home. However, when the case came to trial, the owner was unable to provide the necessary evidence to show that the water damages was caused by something the contractor did or failed to do. Despite the thousands of dollars in damage (*injury*), the owner failed to prove that this contractor was at fault. Just because there is damage does not mean that the person you think is likely responsible is actually responsible. **Fault** must be proven first.

Sometimes the person at *fault* is clear. They conclude that because the other side is plain wrong, they owe the client something. But sometimes, despite how awful the other side acted, there may be no injury. Without injury, there is nothing the law can give you. No injury. No money.

For instance, let's say your neighbor, Jim, agreed to buy your car for $10,000, even though the car is worth only $8,000. Jim is willing to pay the extra $2,000 for reasons that should not matter to you. Right before he is supposed to pay you and receive the car, he tells you he's decided to buy a different car. Jim is definitely at fault for not buying your car, and you feel as if you have been injured. Your car is valued at $8,000, and you were going to make $2,000. Your injury is $2,000 (because you still have the car). But let's say that Jim comes to you and says Bob wants to buy your car instead; he is willing to pay you $9,000 for the car. Your injury is now only $1,000. But if Jim brought Sam over to pay you $12,000 for the car, you would have no injury since you just made an extra $2,000. In each case, Jim is at *"fault"* for breaking your contract. But how much you are injured depends on the entirety of the situation.

These simple stories illustrate the point that both fault and injury are necessary but different. In reality, more facts can complicate the connection between fault and injury. Luckily lawyers are trained to assess both fault and injury and make certain that both exist and are connected.

**Your good lawyer wants you to know** that he/she will work very hard to find the legal injury caused by whomever is at fault. But if no legal fault or legal injury can be found, the law will not have a solution for you.

∽

This chapter is not about the anatomy of a lawsuit. Rather, this section identifies topics that are common in almost all lawsuits and areas that are often misunderstood by clients. The information in this chapter is designed to give you an inside look at some of the realities of what actually happens in the legal system during a lawsuit, so that you can be better equipped to manage your stress and your costs. This information will help you also understand what your lawyer is doing better and help you understand your lawyer's explanations better.

# V. Things You Can Do

*"By failing to prepare, you are preparing to fail."*

BENJAMIN FRANKLIN

Once a lawyer is hired, some clients step back and sit quietly waiting for the lawyer to fix everything. Other clients want to be involved and are ready to roll up their sleeves, dive in while never giving up control. Neither of these situations is ideal.

Yes, a client needs to be involved. At the same time, the client does not need to do *everything*. You've hired the expert—your lawyer—now let your lawyer do what he/she was hired to do. Learn to take direction from your lawyer on how you can help.

That said, there are things you—the client—absolutely must do. You must be prepared to ensure that your lawyer gets everything needed to properly represent you. You must be available, so the lawyer can easily communicate with you. After all, you are the person who has to make the ultimate decisions about your case.

You know your situation better than anyone. You know the facts. Everyone else has to learn your case, and it takes time for anyone else to get up to speed. The easier you make it for your lawyer, the faster your lawyer will catch up to you.

Everything in this section, if followed, will ultimately save you money and relieve stress. Because you will provide your lawyer with everything needed and do what you are asked to do, you will get the most from your lawyer.

## Re-Read Chapter IV

I know you've already read Chapter IV above. But what you can do for yourself is to read it, again. The points covered in Chapter IV are the very points that clients often misunderstand or overlook. By having a better understanding of the points made in Chapter IV, you will become that client that fares better than most. You will be able to make decisions in your case that can save you money and alleviate stress. Your relationship with your lawyer will be better, and you can continue to work as a team.

## Think Settlement: REALLY!

*"Justice is illusive and very expensive."*

From Chapter IV, you learned that settlement is a necessary part of all lawsuits today. Whether you want to or not, you will be sent to some form of settlement discussion before ever reaching trial. I cannot emphasize how important it will be for you to always have in your mind the possibility of settlement and the willingness to discuss settlement.

Today, the United States is viewed by many countries as the most litigious society in the world. We do not need to debate this point. All we need to know is that filing a lawsuit is very easy in this country, and people file lawsuits every day, all day long. If one lawyer tells you that you don't have a case, you can find another who will file the lawsuit for you. It doesn't mean you have a good case. It just means there are lawyers willing to file any lawsuit.

From seeing some of the lawsuits that have been filed, our society has become accustomed to using the legal system to resolve every single possible dispute. This is why the system is overcrowded and overburdened. If you and every litigant read this book and embraced the notion of settlement realistically, a large number of disputes could be and likely would be resolved before any lawsuit was ever filed. And of the number of lawsuits filed, a large number would be resolved shortly after the lawsuit was filed, rather than being dragging along for a year or two, or three, or four costing clients thousands of dollars and years of stress.

If money is no object, and you can be cavalier with your attitude about being involved in the legal system for a few years, perhaps settlement is not anything you need to concern yourself with. But if you are like most people, if you could end your dispute, save money, and move on with your life, wouldn't you rather do that?

If you are seeking "justice" because someone has wronged you, think long and hard about what it was that made you so angry. Will "justice" make it better? Sometimes money will do it. But a bird in a hand is always worth two in the bush. Remember that whenever you are faced with considering settlement.

## Discuss Objectives and Motivation

At the onset of your relationship with your lawyer, discuss your objectives and motivation extensively. During this discussion, you will also learn a great deal about the realities of the legal system. It is important that you and your lawyer are clear about the objectives of your case and have the same goals.

## Set Communication Ground Rules

Every client wants to keep track of his/ her case and wants to be kept informed. You have every right to be in the loop. Hopefully, your lawyer will do his/her best to keep you informed of the progress of your case. But it will help you to know exactly how and when that is going to happen.

There are many ways to keep a client updated on a case. But often the client walks away with one perception of how this will happen while the lawyer, and lawyer's staff, have a different perception. Be clear from the beginning on how and when you can expect to hear from the lawyer.

Never feel you can't call your lawyer, and when you do, you should expect a response within a reasonable time. But calling your lawyer daily to get updates is not the answer and can be costly. Instead, discuss with your lawyer timelines and methods to keep you up to date. If lawyers responded to phone calls and emails as they came in, there would be days when lawyers would get nothing done. Depending on the type of work required, lawyers may need to set aside large chunks of uninterrupted time to concentrate on a pending project. When it's time to work on your case, you want your lawyer to be able to concentrate uninterrupted by other work or other clients.

Typically, law offices will automatically send you copies of papers generated, from correspondence to papers filed with the court, to evidence generated from other sources. Sometimes there is a delay in sending you papers because the lawyer is determining what needs to be done.

An office assistant can sometimes give you a quick status update; however, they are not permitted to discuss legal issues or express opinions about your case.

You can request a timeline of upcoming events, so you can have some gauge. Bear in mind that any timeline a lawyer gives you is just a guideline—often subject to change. Court congestion and backlog, along with what the opposing side may do, impact the timeline significantly.

# Seriously Assume Your Role as Client

## Decision-Making

It's important to understand that in any client/lawyer relationship, some decisions are made by the lawyer while other decisions are yours to make. This means, you need to understand the roles up front and not wait until it's time to make a decision to figure out who is responsible.

Decisions that *materially* impact your rights are yours to make. You have to make the decisions that affect your rights and duties substantially and permanently. Your case, or any portion of your case, cannot be settled without your agreement. Decisions that might cause your fees and costs to increase beyond your fee agreement require your permission (such as hiring a second lawyer to deal with a specialized area). However, the lawyer is there to advise you and help you with the decision-making process.

Decisions that impact how the case moves forward, such as tactics and strategies, should be left to your lawyer. He/She is the expert. Procedural matters which do not substantially and permanently affect your rights are decisions your lawyer makes. These may include when to set hearings, continue hearings, obtaining extensions from deadlines, whether and what motions to file, and how to manage discovery and evidence gathering. You are paying your expert lawyer to facilitate the process. If the decisions are significant, your lawyer should discuss the matter with you in advance.

## Prepare Your Facts

Earlier, I mentioned how important the facts in your case are. They are so important that it's worth taking the time to write them down chronologically for your lawyer. From your lawyer's point of view, there is no such thing as "too many facts or details." A lawyer can read through facts and determine which ones are very important, which ones might become important, and which ones are not important at all. Give your lawyer all the details and empower him/her to decide.

As stated, organize your facts as a chronology of events. Be as precise as possible with key players. Note who was present. Provide key statements. State who said what. Identify places, times, and dates. Use whatever format you are most comfortable with. Here are some suggestions to create this chronology in a way that may be useful for a lawyer:

1. Put dates or date ranges. If dates are important to your situation, try to be as accurate as possible.
2. Include times or time of day if possible. (day or night?)
3. If the physical surroundings are important, include weather conditions. (It had snowed the night before; it was raining hard; it was a sunny, warm day, etc.)
4. Include what you personally know because you *personally* observed the event and include where and who was present. Describe the situation to demonstrate that you personally observed the event. For example, "I was at the building when the inspector arrived. I followed the inspector to the basement. While we were in the basement, we looked in the northwest corner and saw water dripping and the inspector said, 'Now, that's not good.'"
5. In the chronology, include the names and contact information of all witnesses. This includes anyone who might know anything about the event, facts, or background. Provide any potentially useful information. And include what it is that the person knows or claims to know.

6. Include what the opposition may be is saying and/or is claiming about the situation, if you know. For example, "Brown says that I told him I would reduce the price."

7. Include what you know because you learned it (heard it) from someone else and include that person's name and relationship to you. For example: "My neighbor Sue told me that my landlord came to the house on Sunday morning when I wasn't home. She said she saw the landlord enter the front door, and he was in there for about an hour."

Number seven trips people up all the time. I hear people discount what they "heard" by saying, "Well, that's just hearsay so it doesn't matter." Rather than you deciding what does or does not matter, include it. Let the lawyer decide what is relevant. Often the critical piece of evidence is found in what someone else told you. By including this information, you allow the lawyer to decide what can be used and figure out how to make it usable.

## Organize Your Documents

Documents are included in your facts.

Every piece of paper you have acquired relating to your situation, problem, or desired outcome is considered a fact and something that your lawyer needs to see.

When the lawyer asks for your documents, bring everything. Don't make the decision about what is important and what is not important. Lawyers are trained to look at a lot of documents and quickly figure out what's important and what is not. Sometimes the key piece of paper is a napkin on which something was scribbled.

You have the choice of bringing papers haphazardly thrown into a box or organized in a manner that makes it easy for the lawyer to review. Having some organization not only helps the lawyer in reviewing your case, but this also helps you to make sure you have everything.

For example, I had a client once who had several banker boxes of documents. But before she brought the documents to me, she organized everything into 3-ring binders which came in chronological order. Each binder had a time period on the spine with a notation as to its relevance. The documents were tabbed, indexed, and each binder had a table of contents. I have to say, it was one remarkable set of binders. Needless to say, reviewing her documents took considerably less time than usual. I would not expect most clients to do what she did, but it made my job easier and certainly helped keep costs down.

There is more than one way to organize any set of documents. You can organize chronologically or by subject matter. It likely depends on the type of situation you have, the type of case, or the type of problem. The point is to be able to find the critical documents quickly. Typically, after organizing documents, you will find that there are some papers that just don't seem to fit into your system of organization. Just place those into a "miscellaneous" category, but include them.

Next, compare your documents to your chronology of facts. This will help you identify if you are missing documents. Doing so may trigger a memory of some fact you mistakenly omitted.

Do not be surprised that whatever way you choose may be reorganized by your lawyer. Ultimately, the organization must suit the lawyer's way of thinking and how the lawyer works, and reorganization may become necessary. But it is much easier to reorganize a well organized set of documents than to organize the documents from a pile of disorganized papers. You can also ask your lawyer if he /she has a preference on how the documents are organized and follow those instructions.

I am always impressed when a client presents me with exceptionally organized information. You would be surprised by the high percentage of clients who do not put effort into these tasks. Your lawyer will be immediately pleased to have you as a client if you start off this way. A happy lawyer is a good lawyer.

## Stay Organized

Staying organized means checking your mail every day. It means opening every piece of mail every day. It means checking your telephone messages daily. It means checking your email regularly. And it means gathering new information that comes your way and getting it to your lawyer immediately.

During the time you and your lawyer are working on your case, developments occur. For instance, sometimes you will learn the name of a new witness. Or an important document will appear. Perhaps you'll hear about some facts (even if it's "hearsay"). Gather this information and give it to your lawyer *right away*. Oftentimes, clients avoid doing this because they don't want to get charged for another phone call with the lawyer. You don't need to call your lawyer to do this. Type up the information, put it together with the document, and email it to the lawyer (or the staff person assigned to your case). Drop it off at the office. Or even call your lawyer! Frankly, the cost of a short telephone call is cheap compared to what will happen if you don't communicate with your lawyer about new developments.

Imagine your lawyer working on your case. Maybe he is drafting a contract or researching your case. You get information that will change what the lawyer is doing. If you don't share this information with your lawyer, your lawyer is proceeding, and you are being charged for this work. Once the lawyer knows about the new information, the lawyer may have to redo something—or everything. The longer you wait to tell your lawyer, the more it will cost you. Now imagine how much *more* stress you will suffer because your fees just increased, and you're kicking yourself for not staying organized.

## Just Answer the Question PLEASE!

*It's not your job anymore to convince anyone of the rightness of your case or your position.* In fact, it's counter-productive. Let your lawyer do this. I suspect many lawyers have emphasized this over and over; it's a message that's hard to get through to clients.

Lawyers spend time preparing their clients for depositions. At the deposition, the opposing lawyer is going to ask you a lot of questions. These questions and your answers will be taken down by a court reporter. The purpose is for the lawyer taking the deposition (the other guy) to find out what you have to say. The benefit to that lawyer (the other guy) is by having you say more, the lawyer learns more about what you might say. The more you say, the more the lawyer has to "trip you up" later.

But it is the other lawyer's job to figure out all the right questions to ask. It is not your job to volunteer information. Sometimes the other lawyer fails to ask all the right questions and leaves without everything he/she needs. That's not your problem.

If you are in a deposition and your lawyer kicks you under the table, don't say "ouch." Your lawyer is telling you to stop talking, to stop volunteering information that goes beyond the question asked.

When I handled litigation and trial cases, I loved it when the opposing client started talking excessively. That person was giving me more than I could have anticipated. Meanwhile, the lawyer sitting next to that client is cringing and trying to get the client to stop talking. If the opposing lawyer was questioning my client, and this was happening, I'd be the one sitting next to my client cringing and kicking my client under the table. This seems to happen no matter how much I instructed my client in advance. So please, *just answer the question* and do not volunteer anything else.

*Less is more.* You're not there to tell your story or convince the lawyer how right you are. If the lawyer walks out not knowing anything, that's fine. We are not there to educate. Yet, when clients have an opportunity to talk, they talk. Now that you are reading this, let's give your trusted lawyer a break, shall we? Tell your lawyer that you read this, highlighted it and understand that when anyone, besides your lawyer in the lawyer's office, is asking you any questions, you only say as much as is necessary to answer the specific question, and you are not there to educate anyone or convince them of your case, your situation, or your rightness.

And if you end up in trial, even when your lawyer is asking questions, you simply answer each question—*just answer the question*—and no more. If you are testifying at trial and your lawyer is making an exaggerated stern face, stop talking. Although at a trial, your side's job is to convince a judge or a jury about the rightness of your position, let your lawyer orchestrate how that will happen. Your lawyer is the one with the expertise, experience, and talent that you are paying for. Don't feel you need to blurt out everything all at once, which can be counter-productive.

I know you want to tell your whole story all at once. I know you want to convince the judge or jury you are right, and the other side is wrong. I know you have a lot to say, and your mind is racing. Restrain yourself. Do what your lawyer tells you and *just answer the question.*

## Be Courteous

There was a time when lawyers would bring boxes of candy to the courthouse and leave them for the clerks during the holidays. This was done just to be nice and show appreciation. That practice stopped a long time ago because it was perceived by some that perhaps some lawyers were doing it to obtain favors from the courthouse staff. How lawyers get cooperation from courthouse staff is to be consistently courteous to them. Believe me, clerks remember the lawyers who are polite and courteous.

So it goes for the client. *Always* be nice to everyone on the lawyer's staff and in the courts, if applicable. These personnel can be crucial to solving problems. A little courtesy goes a long way. Most lawyers are very protective of their staff because most lawyers have dealt with at least one client who has been unkind to a staff member. The last thing I want is for my receptionist to run into my office crying because a client was rude.

Your reputation as a client is important. It's important in continuing to develop that relationship of trust with your lawyer. A lawyer is capable of breaking the trust with you. But you, too, are capable of breaking that trust with the lawyer and his office personnel. Preserve that trust in every way you can.

## Opposition

> *"The trial of a lawsuit is not a game where the spoils of victory go to the clever and technical regardless of the merits, but a method devised by a civilized society to settle peaceably and justly disputes between litigants."*
>
> SIMON V. CITY AND COUNTY OF SAN FRANCISCO
> (1947) 79 CAL.APP.2D 590

Many years ago, a colleague of mine gave me the reference to the above quote. Since then, I have used this quote in a number of papers I have filed with the court to remind the court and opposing counsel that lawsuits are not a game. At best, lawsuits are designed to be the method we use to *peaceably* and *justly* resolve disputes. When I take a case, I hope that a good lawyer is my opposing counsel. Good lawyers understand the ideals outlined in this quote, and even if we disagree on points, and even though we are hired to take opposing positions, we know that rudeness, backstabbing, or gamesmanship do not aid in the final outcome or resolution. In fact, such negative behavior often interferes with quick resolution. Good lawyers are capable of having a discussion with opposing views without getting personal or angry. That's why you hired your good lawyer.

Be calm and courteous despite how angry you are with the other side. Adding fuel to the fire does not help you resolve your case any sooner. Stay focused on the goal to get your problem resolved, so you can move on. Don't act in ways that just irk the other side, giving them the chance to dig in their heels even more. The longer your case takes to resolve, the more stress you will suffer, and the more money it will cost you.

## Beware The Over-Traps

I define the "over-traps" as the consequence of over-reading, over-thinking, and over-discussing your case. They involve the things clients do *unnecessarily* to increase stress. They are of little, to no, benefit for you, your lawyer, or your case. By addressing them here, I hope to help mitigate some of the stress you may experience.

Many studies have shown that the mind does not always fully distinguish between what is real and what is imaginary. Perhaps you have heard about the basketball team study done many years ago (the methods and topic of which have been studied many times since). One group was asked to practice foul shots every day for a set period of time. Another group was not allowed to practice physically but was asked to practice only in their imagination making foul shots for the same amount of time. A control group was not allowed to practice at all. At the end of a month, both the group that had physically practiced and the group that had only visually practiced had improved similarly. On the other hand, the group that did not practice at all did not show any improvement. Hence began more studies of how the brain does not distinguish between imagination and reality.

**Over-traps** are behaviors that trigger imaginary concerns. The imaginary concerns will cause the same reaction in your mind and body that real life stressors create. Once your lawyer tells you what the risks and concerns are, obsessively researching, thinking, and discussing your case may create unnecessary concerns creating more anxiety and stress.

Despite being warned not to over-read, over-think, or over-talk your case, lawyers know that clients just can't help it. If you find yourself in the over-trap, you should call your lawyer for another real risk-assessment and reality check on your case. You need to let him/her know that you have worked yourself up into an over-trap situation. Lawyers want to help you, but you need to communicate your concerns/anxieties.

**Note**: If your lawyer has asked you to gather information, you may experience some stress as well. This cannot be helped, but in doing what your lawyer has specifically asked you to do, you are not in an over-trap situation.

## Over-Researching

In hiring a lawyer, you are trusting him/her to take care of matters. This allows you to loosen the reigns and relax a little. Some clients just can't help researching the Internet for laws, cases, and blogs that might mention similarities to their cases. We understand clients want to be proactive. We often encourage this. But when done excessively, a client may read inapplicable information causing unnecessary worry. Oftentimes, over-researching becomes an obsession, and a client begins delivering documents, briefs, and information to the lawyer, expecting the lawyer to read it all. Your lawyer does not have time to read all of your research. Your lawyer is conducting his/her own specific and relevant research on your case already. You don't want to pay your lawyer to read volumes of pages printed off the Internet.

**Over-researching can lead to poor resourcing.** Information from the Internet can be misleading and therefore of little use. The section entitled, "Do You Need a Lawyer?" describes the difference between *legal advice* and *legal information*. What you find on the internet is legal information, not legal advice. If you read blogs, you may read one lawyer's opinion about a case, and it's just that—an opinion. This does not mean, however, that you ignore possible pertinent information at your disposal.

Sometimes you will hear important information that should be shared with your lawyer. For instance, we were representing a client against a small company and were in the middle of a lawsuit. One day, our client heard through the grapevine that this small company was going to file bankruptcy. Our client told us, and we began watching the bankruptcy filings. We picked up the bankruptcy filing as soon as it happened. This was useful information as it was specific to the opponent.

**Over-researching is a poor use of time.** To illustrate, in California, every criminal defendant has an automatic right to appeal after a conviction. In my appellate practice, I sometimes represent criminal clients who are in prison. In some of those cases, I receive mail from my clients containing 20-30 pages of research that the client has done in the prison law library. These pages are often hand written, verbatim copies of cases and other texts the client has found in the library. Although I tell my clients that I have access to the same books and that a case name or page from a book would suffice, I continue to receive the single-spaced handwritten tiny script of texts from books, *word for word*. Given their situation, I understand that copying the texts from books may provide a sense of hope and make use of excessive free time. However, I suggest to you that it's not the wisest choice and actually might greatly increase your stress.

## Over-Thinking

Overthinking results in the *What if? syndrome*. It's when clients start imagining unlikely and unfounded consequences, usually negative ones.

"What if the bank doesn't want to settle?"

"What if the lender starts foreclosure?"

"What if the regulatory agency says 'no'?"

"What if the other side lies?"

The *what ifs?* are endless. In some cases, yes, the *what if?* can manifest. But until it happens, it is pure conjecture.

I learned this lesson, oddly, from my oncologist. I was diagnosed with cancer sixteen years ago. As soon as I heard that I had cancer, my mind went racing to all the *what ifs? What if it's so advanced they can't do anything about it? What if chemo-therapy doesn't work? What if radiation doesn't work? What if after surgery, I don't go into remission?* And so on. As I rattled off several of these concerns, my oncologist reached across the table, gently took my hands into his and said to me, "Don't worry. We'll cross each bridge when, and if, we get there. For now, let's just start with the first step." He managed to calm me. I had surgery, and he removed the cancer. I did not have to have any therapy, and have been cancer free since. None of those *what ifs?* ever manifested. He saved me from excessive worrying.

Yes, we must plan for practical contingencies. However, your lawyer may often tell you, "Let's wait on that until … [we take so-and-so's deposition … we get the ruling from the court on our motion … we get the evidence in from the title company ….]

Save yourself from worrying about legal problems that don't exist, yet.

## Over-Discussing

This section is more of a *word of caution*. Most people want to avoid legal disputes. Few want to spend their life energy, time, and money in litigation. But sometimes it can't be helped.

When we are upset, it is natural and normal to want to talk to someone about it. Clients often turn to spouses, children, relatives, neighbors, friends, hairdressers, and softball pals, etc. to talk about their situation in an attempt to validate feelings. Typically you will re-hash points that are at the center of dispute. Your talk may involve criticizing the other side for being unreasonable. The other side may very well be unreasonable. But talking to everyone and anyone about it is not going to change how the other side acts. Nor is it going to change what your lawyer can do, or the facts in the case. It almost always leads to more stress.

∼

There are many ways you, the client, can help yourself to control your cost, your stress level, and be the most help to your lawyer. Now that you have hired your good lawyer and understand better how the legal system works, it is important that you also stay involved in a way that helps your case. This chapter outlines some fundamental ways you can have control in your case and be involved while not interfering with what you have hired your good lawyer to do. I hope this chapter gives you some perspective on how your role as a client fits well with the role of your good lawyer so that you can work as a team to solve problems.

# VI. Conclusion

*"Courage is what it takes to stand up and speak; courage is also what it takes to sit down and listen."*

Winston Churchill

This book is a primer for clients headed toward legal action.

No lawyer can spend the time to tell a client everything in this book at the beginning of a case. Yet, I believe that every good lawyer wants their clients to know everything in this book. I wrote the book in an effort to mitigate some of your concerns and educate you about the process—to make things easier for both you and your lawyer.

By reading this book, you now have some understanding about how things work in the legal world. You are informed in advance about things that might happen. When anything in this book does happen in your case, your lawyer will explain it. But, even if you are maddened to some extent about what is happening, at least you won't be surprised. Instead, you will be somewhat prepared to listen to your lawyer's explanation and perhaps better understand. You will know that you and your lawyer are on the same team no matter what anyone else is doing.

It is important to note that one of the most expensive things you can do is switch lawyers in the middle of a lawsuit. Your finding a good lawyer and keeping that relationship strong is essential to saving money and reducing stress. Your finding a good lawyer is critical to getting the most out of your lawyer. But, even with a good lawyer found, I wrote this book so that you would have the information necessary so that you will keep your good lawyer to the end.

This book is *not* a substitute for consulting a lawyer and *not* a substitute for listening to your lawyer. Find your good lawyer; then trust your good lawyer. Good luck!

# Appendix

## Resources

**State Court Websites.** Almost every state now has a Court Website that is a central location from which you can branch out to more local courts. At these sites, you can find a great deal of **legal information** including more about the legal profession, the court system, location of courts, publications and brochures on how to do things yourself, forms and rules. *Go to any search engine and type in the state name and courts (example: California Courts) and you'll find this central court website.* Some states do not have a central site, but virtually every type of court has a website where you will find valuable legal information. Often the information found at these websites can provide you with some background and insight before you see your lawyer.

**Federal Court Websites.** The federal courts system involves District Courts, Circuit Courts and ultimately the United States Supreme Court. The federal system has been online longer than state courts and has extensive information about its system, legal information and cases. *Go to any search engine and type in "federal courts" or "US Courts," and you will find links to federal court websites.*

**Bar Associations.** Every state and many cities and counties have bar associations. These are the organizations to which lawyers are members. Some states have an "integrated" bar association meaning every lawyer in the state is required to be a member. California is one of those states. Every lawyer licensed in California must be a member of the California Bar Association and is subject to its rules and disciplinary measures. Some states have "volunteer" bar associations where lawyers are not required to be a member. The American Bar Association is a volunteer association not associated with any state and serves lawyers nationally. The websites to these bar associations have a lot of information about lawyers, the legal system and general legal information. *Go to any search engine and type in "bar association" and the state/county/city, and you'll find a link to the a bar association.*

## Lawyer's Code of Ethics

No book about lawyers would be complete without referring to the Code of Ethics that govern the duties and actions of lawyers. Every state has a Code of Professional Responsibility.

Every state, except California, has adopted the Model Rules of Professional Responsibility drafted by the American Bar Association. You can find the Model Rules at The American Bar Association Web Site (www.americanbar.org). If you are looking for your particular State's Code of Ethics, I recommend you go to your state's actual rules. Even when a state adopts the American Bar Association's Model Rules, a state can make changes within the Model Rules to suit the state. California has adopted an extensive set of Rules of Professional Responsibility. These can be found at the California State Bar Association Web Site (http://www.calbar.ca.gov/).

The rules governing lawyer conduct have changed over the years. These rules are changed to reflect the world in which lawyers work. In the 1960s, no lawyer even considered advertising because it was against the "Canons of Professional Ethics" developed by the American Bar Association in 1908. Interestingly, before 1908, lawyers were advertising (quite a bit actually). In 1908, the American Bar Association believed that advertising made lawyers appear unprofessional, so it was banned. Then in the 1970s, this ban was challenged in an Arizona case, and the United States Supreme Court struck down the complete ban on advertising, while allowing State Bars to regulate advertising to protect the public from false advertising. The 1970s saw a boom in advertising by lawyers which has continued to today. This change required every state to develop rules that govern lawyer advertising.

But in the 1970s, no one anticipated the internet, emails, document preparation, and storage on electronic devices. The world of information, which used to be on paper with carbon copies (some of you may not even know what that is), produced on typewriters, forever began changing in the 1980s. Now, rules relating to electronic production and storage are required.

The integrity of business, privacy of personal affairs, and the attorney-client privilege all face an every-morphing computer age where storage, hacks, easy reproduction, easy modification, easy deleting and accidental electronic disclosures threaten the protective pillars that have been hallmarks of the legal profession.

This section is included to remind you that the legal profession has and always will need to modify the rules that govern lawyers because the world keeps changing. But the changes are meant to protect the legal system, the profession, and the client to preserve integrity. The topic of ethics is a complicated subject for another book entirely. But know that the legal profession as a whole is forever vigilant in the watch. As indicated above, because the wheels of justice tend to turn on the slower side, sometimes the profession responds slowly to the change, but it inevitably responds.

# Glossary

This glossary is intended to describe some of the terms used in the book. This glossary in no way covers all the techinical legal terms you may hear or read in your encounter with the legal system.

**Answer/Response.** If you are the person who has been sued, the first written response that you must file in court is the Answer or Response. What documents are called will vary from state to state.

**Appellate Practice.** Appellate practice refers to work that is handled in courts higher than the court in which most original proceedings are filed. In some cases, the original proceeding may be an administrative hearing such as agency hearings (e.g. Labor Commissions) or county government (e.g., Board of Supervisor hearings). If you don't like the results from those proceedings, you may be able to "appeal" the results to a higher authority or tribunal which may be the regular trial court in your county. If the original proceedings was a lawsuit filed in the trial court, you would "appeal" the results to the next higher tribunal which is typically an appellate court. The highest appellate court in the United States is the United State Supreme Court. Each state has its own court structure and may call the various levels of courts different names, but the structure is similar among the states.

**Alternative Dispute Resolution (ADR).** ADR is any method of resolving a dispute other than resorting to the court system. Many forms of ADR exist today. Some organizations have ADR companies they use to handle dispute resolution. Retired judges have come together to offer ADR services to anyone and especially to lawyers and their clients to help resolve legal disputes faster than the legal system can. Typically, the parties to a lawsuit will agree to share the cost of ADR. Today, many contracts include language which obligates the parties to first attempt ADR before a lawsuit can be filed.

**Arbitration.** Arbitration is a form of ADR in which the parties will present their case to a neutral arbitrator. The arbitrator will listen to each side of the case, look at the evidence, and make a decision. The arbitrator acts as the judge in the arbitration process. The benefits to arbitration include speed and informality. One can agree beforehand to accept the arbitration decision as the final say or agree that the either party can reject the decision and proceed with a lawsuit.

**Associate Counsel.** In some cases, your lawyer may want to and need to hire a specialist lawyer. If a specialist lawyer is called in, while keeping your lawyer, the specialist lawyer will be an associate counsel. An example may be your trial lawyer hiring an appellate law specialist when your case is appealed. Both your trial lawyer and the specialist will be representing you, but your trial lawyer will defer to the specialist until that part of the case is completed. If this happens, just be sure you understand the fee arrangements.

**Calendars.** In the legal system, calendars typically refer to the calendar of the court. Each judge has his/her calendar. That calendar, like everyone else's calendar, contains scheduled events. For example, one judge might have a motions hearing calendar every Monday from nine to noon. In order to make certain that the judge only sits in the courtroom from nine until noon, the court clerk will limit the number of cases that can be scheduled to be heard on a particular day. Once the limit has been filed, the court clerk will not allow other cases to be scheduled for that date and time period. What this means to you is that despite you and your lawyer wanting to calendar a motion for a particular day, the calendar may be full, and the next available date may be farther away than is desirable. Court congestion influences the judges' calendars, which directly impact how quickly your case can be heard.

**Co-Counsel**. In some cases, your side of a lawsuit might have more than one person. However, the same lawyer may not be able to represent all the persons on that one side because of a possible conflict of interest. When parties of the same side have to have different lawyers, those lawyers are referred to as co-counsel.

**Complaint/Petition**. If you are the person who wants to file a lawsuit, the first written papers that you must file in court is the Complaint, Petition or similarly called document. What documents are called will vary from state to state.

**Courthouse Personnel**.

**Clerks** make up the largest population in the court system. Clerks take your papers when you file them with the court, manage the calendaring system, maintain the files, collect payment, review documents for accuracy and completeness. Each judge has his/ her own clerk who manages a multitude of tasks in the courtroom and for the judge. Clerks are not lawyers or judges. Clerks are not authorized to give legal advice to anyone. They can, however, share legal information. Clerks have been instructed and trained to tell you that you need to consult with a lawyer if you need legal advice.

**Stenographic Court Reporters** are the people who take down every word said in the courtroom. When asked, what was said in the courtroom will be transcribed and the transcript of what was said can be made available to the judge, the lawyers and the parties to the case. Historically, court reporters were always present anytime a judge was sitting in the courtroom, and lawyers and parties were present to discuss or argue a case. In some jurisdictions, due to budgetary constraints, you must ask and pay for the presence of a court reporter in cases in which the law does not mandate their presence. In those jurisdictions, this is now an added cost to litigation.

**Bailiffs** are typically law enforcement officers who sit in the courtroom. The bailiff's role is to keep law and order in the courtroom, assuring that everyone follows the rules. One of the primary functions of the bailiff is to keep the judge safe.

**Judges** are the persons in the black robes who will be making decisions that impact your case. A judge, in most instances, was formerly a lawyer. However, judges give up the right to give legal advice once they become a judge and so long as he/she remains a judge. The role of the lawyer is to advocate for one side or the other. The role of the judge is to listen attentively with judicial decorum to all sides. Judges do not make the law. Judges listen to evidence and must decide what the facts are. Then judges must determine what law applies to the facts. A judge must then apply the law to the facts and reach a decision.

- **Defendant.** If you are the person against whom a claim has been made, you are the defendant (or respondent). You might see the terminology "Cross-defendant" sometimes. This refers to someone who started out as a plaintiff or complainant and the other side brought a counter-claim. So now the plaintiff/complainant is now also a cross-defendant.

- **Fault.** Fault (technical legal definition) is a negligent or intentional act or failure to act in a manner that the law recognizes as placing a burden on the actor to be responsible for the results caused by that act or omission. Even if someone "causes" the result, that person may not necessarily be held "at fault." And even if you strongly suspect that someone caused the result, the law requires proof to meet its very technical definition of fault. The concept of fault has been and will continue to be a question that is heavily litigated.

**Hearing.** In the legal system, a hearing refers to a dispute brought to the attention of the court which is not a trial. Topics can range from whether your lawsuit is in the correct court to whether a trial is even needed for a judge to decide the outcome of the case.

**Injury.** Injury refers to harm suffered. The harm may be to a person (physically or emotionally), a person's rights, reputation, or to property. The law recognizes many types of harms. "Damages" and "loss" are synonymous with injury.

**Judgment.** Typically there is only one judgment per case. The judgment refers to the final document that puts an end to the case in the trial court. This is the judge's decision.

**Law Office Personnel.**

**Receptionist.** This person's primary role is to greet persons who enter the office, answer the telephone, and sort the mail. Depending on the law office, the receptionist may have other duties, as well. Most receptionist roles do not include having specific information relating to a client or the client's case. Receptionists also do not typically exercise discretion about what information to relay to callers. In many law offices, especially big firms, receptionists have no information about any particular case.

**Legal Secretaries.** Everyone knows what a secretary does. But that is why I titled this person the "legal" secretary. Legal secretaries are highly specialized secretaries. Most have been trained in school to understand the legal system and how it works and are highly trained to process documents efficiently and quickly. Not only can they type quickly, they know how to maneuver through the court system. Top legal secretaries can be the right arm of a lawyer, and lawyers will rely heavily on good legal secretaries to help process cases.

**Paralegals**. Paralegals are legal technicians who have been trained to understand the complexity of legal procedures and processing of cases. In some cases, top end legal secretaries have the skills of trained paralegals. In a law office paralegals serve a important role in processing information and documents so that a lawyer's time is dedicated to research and analysis of cases and law. In some jurisdictions, paralegals have been given the authority to act independent of a lawyer in performing limited tasks such as filling out court forms. *Word to the wise: paralegals are not lawyers and are not authorized to give legal advice.*

**Law Clerk**. Law clerks are typically law students. They are hired to conduct research directed by a lawyer. Law clerks provide a great service to lawyers by conducting basic research. Meanwhile, the law clerk is receiving training for his/her future as a lawyer.

**Office Administrator**. The office administrator is the person who runs the administrative or business side of the law office. Clients often do not see this person. This person is in charge of staff issues, insurance, paying the rent, and making sure the office is running smoothly. The larger the firm or staff, the greater the need for someone in this position.

**Lawyer**. Lawyers in a law firm can have additional titles such as Associate, Junior Associate, Senior Associate, Junior Partner, Senior Partner, Partner, and Of Counsel. All of these folks are lawyers licensed to practice law and all can give you legal advice. All can be hired to help you with a case. These titles reflect mostly the comparative level of experience among the group of lawyers in the law firm and the financial arrangements they have amongst themselves. For purposes of hiring a lawyer, typically, you will hire one of the more senior lawyers while junior lawyers are assigned to work on the case. In smaller firms, you will find less titles.

**Legal Advice.** Legal advice includes determining and counseling a client on what the law, consisting of statutes, codes, regulations, rules and cases (precedent), means, and how it applies to a client's situation. Only a lawyer can give someone legal advice. A lawyer will give out legal advice only after the lawyer has developed a relationship with a client. Legal advice is not given out generally. Legal advice necessarily is specific to a particular client's situation.

**Legal Information.** Legal information is general information about the legal system, the law, and process which is readily available. The best resources for reliable legal information are court, bar association and lawyer's websites. At a lawyer's website, you will find valuable legal information but you will not find legal advice.

**Mediation.** Mediation is a form of Alternate Dispute Resolution (ADR). Mediation is a settlement negotiation. Parties typically split the cost of the mediator. The mediator is a neutral person who hears both side of the dispute and attempts to find the common ground in order to resolve the dispute. Compromise is a key component of mediation because it is a key component of any settlement. The benefit of mediation is that all parties have some control over the outcome because the outcome of mediation is an agreement. Mediation requires that all parties agree to the resolution.

**Motions.** A motion is a formal request made to the judge. The judge consider motions and makes a ruling in the form of a order or judgment. Motions can be made any time, before, during or after trial. Motions can include any request from asking for a continuance to bringing an end to the case. Motions can be written as well as oral. Rules and procedures are in place that govern how and when particular motions can be made. In a typical case, several motions will be made throughout the case while the case is being prepared for trial.

**Opposing Counsel.** Opposing counsel is the lawyer hired by the other side.

**Orders.** Decisions made by judges are called orders. When judges make decision on motions, they issue orders. Orders do not, in themselves, bring an end to the case. However, if the order is the final decision on a case, it will be followed by the judgment, which is the final decision in the case.

**Plaintiff/Complainant/Petitioner.** This is the person who started the lawsuit. You might see the terminology "Cross-plaintiff / cross-complainant" sometimes. This refers to someone who was the defendant when the lawsuit was filed, but now has brought a counter-claim.

**Substitute Counsel.** If you decided you wanted to terminate your relationship with your lawyer and hire a different lawyer while a lawsuit was pending, you would need to file documents with the court to show that change in lawyer. During this process, your new lawyer is the substitute counsel.

**Trial.** This is the ultimate forum to win or lose the war. Trial can be in front of a jury or in front of a single judge. Juries are not allowed in all cases. Each state has rules about which type of cases can be heard by a jury and which must be heard by only a judge. For example, physical injury cases are almost always heard by juries. But divorces and other family matters are usually reserved for judge trials only. Jury trials are much more expensive. You must pay for the jury. Jury trials take much longer. You have to allow time to pick the jury and the lawyers and judge must spent a lot of time drafting instructions to the jury on what the law is. Trial preparation and presentation must be much more detailed than when trying a case to a judge only. Even if you are entitled to a jury trial, you and your lawyer must consider whether it is wiser to have your case heard by a judge. These decisions involve your lawyer's assessment of your case based your lawyer's experience and understanding of the legal system in which your case is pending.

# About the Author

Francine R. Tone is a lawyer, licensed to practice law in the State of California and is the managing partner of the law firm of Tone & Tone, Attorneys at Law. She is also an Appellate Law Specialist, certified by the California State Bar Board of Legal Specialization. She has also sat as a judge *pro tem* for almost 20 years.

Ms. Tone has been practicing law since 1989. During the early years, she was a trial attorney handling business and real estate matters and was often hired by family law and probate lawyers, as well as lawyers in other legal disciplines, to handle real estate related litigation.

Today, Ms. Tone's firm handles appeals from a variety of fields and handles business and real estate litigation and transactions. Ms. Tone now primarily devotes her practice to appeals and providing services to trial attorneys to develop and preserve technical legal issues for trial and for pursuing or defending an appeal.

In addition to her firm's own experience with clients over the years, her extensive involvement in the relationship of other lawyers with their clients has led her to produce this book.

**Notes**

## Notes

# Notes

Made in the USA
San Bernardino, CA
12 October 2016